*THE MASTER DIVER
AND UNDERWATER SPORTSMAN*

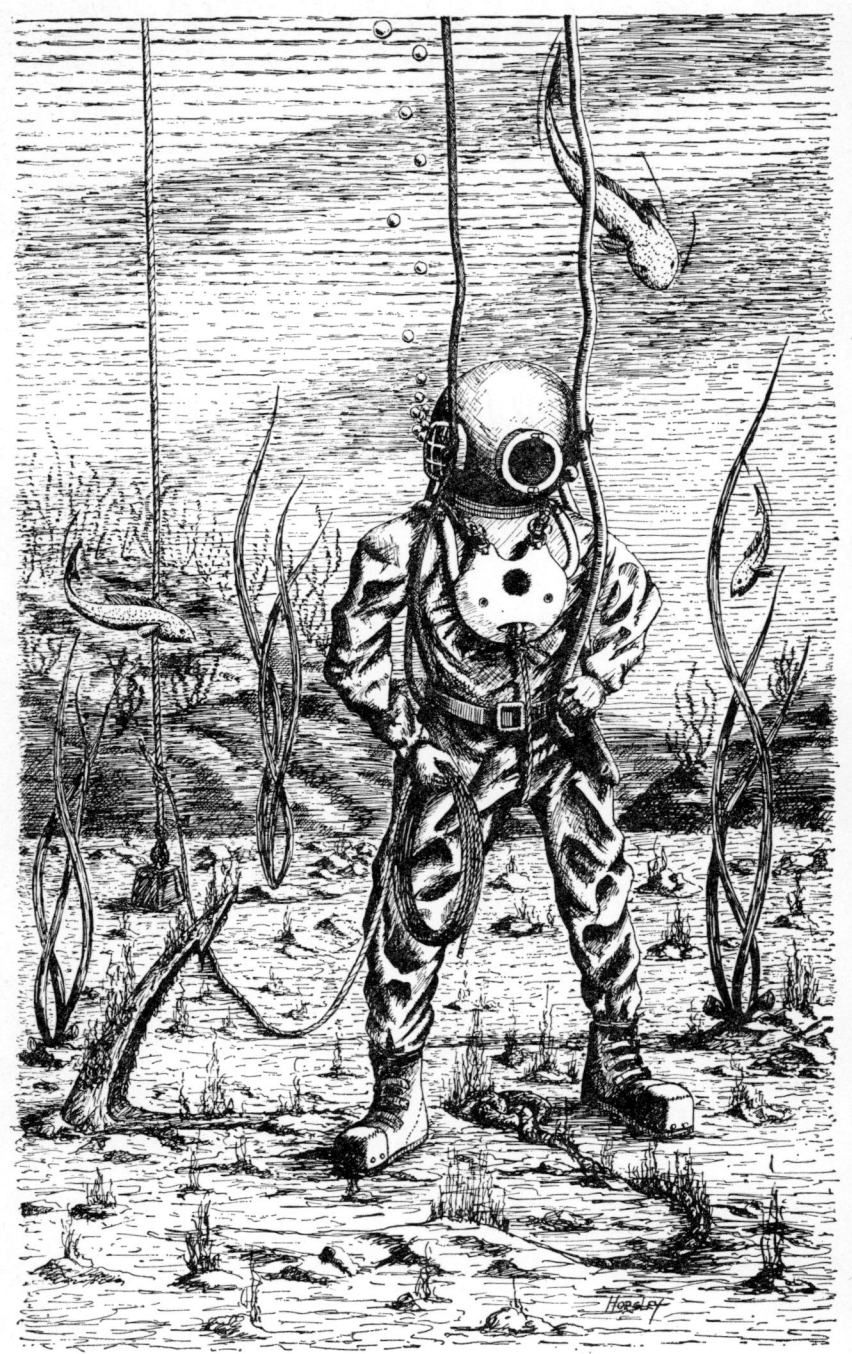

The Standard Diver

THE MASTER DIVER AND UNDERWATER SPORTSMAN

by Captain T. A. Hampton
AFC, CEng, AMRINA

ARCO PUBLISHING COMPANY, INC.
New York

A substantially revised edition, with additional material and completely new illustrations, of the book first published in 1955 (second edition 1962)

Published by ARCO PUBLISHING COMPANY, Inc.
219 Park Avenue South, New York, N.Y. 10003

© T. A. HAMPTON 1970

All Rights Reserved. No part of this
publication may be reproduced, stored
in a retrieval system, or transmitted,
in any form or by any means, electronic,
mechanical, photocopying, recording or
otherwise, without the prior permission
of the publishers.

Library of Congress Catalog Card Number 79-121369

ISBN 0-668-02353-8

Printed in Great Britain

CONTENTS

Chapter		Page
1	THE MAN-FISH	11
	The swim-diver · diving physiology	
2	TO BE FOREWARNED	20
	Depth pressures · the bends · nitrogen narcosis · oxygen poisoning · carbon dioxide contamination · carbon monoxide poisoning	
3	THE MEANS	31
	Breathing apparatus · compressed air apparatus	
4	AQUALUNG TRAINING	40
	Apparatus · first lesson · second lesson · practice	
5	OXYGEN REBREATHING APPARATUS	51
	Apparatus · use of apparatus	
6	STANDARD DIVING APPARATUS	59
	Dressing the diver · first lesson · second lesson	
7	AIR SUPPLY	73
	Hand pumps · power compressors · high-pressure compressors	
8	DEEP DIVING AND COAST DIVING	79
	Mixture diving · coast diving	
9	PROTECTIVE CLOTHING	87
	Ear pressure compensators · repairs	
10	FISHES AND CRUSTACEA	101
	Lobsters · crabs · underwater fishing	
11	THE SUBMARINE SEASCAPE	118
	Seaweeds · photography · visibility	

12	UNDERWATER WORK	page 129
13	UNDERWATER CUTTING AND WELDING Gas cutting · oxy-arc cutting · arc welding	133
14	UNDERWATER BLASTING Explosives and fuses · detonators · electric firing · delay detonators · exploders · rock excavation · removal of sand and silt · blasting trenches · precautions	139
15	SEAMANSHIP FOR DIVERS The magnetic compass · tides and tidal currents · position at sea · buoyage · rope	161
16	ARTIFICIAL RESPIRATION	175
	DECOMPRESSION TABLES	179
	APPENDIX Manufacturers of Diving Equipment	186
	DIVING DATA	188
	INDEX	189

ILLUSTRATIONS

PLATES	Page
Twin-cylinder aqualung and dry suit	17
Section of HP alloy cylinder (*Midland Diving Equipment Ltd*)	17
Single-cylinder aqualung	18
Twin-cylinder aqualung (*Submarine Products Ltd*)	18
Single hose reducer and demand valve	35
Merlin Mk VI demand valve	35
Demand valves used for surface supply	36
Triple-cylinder rig (*Submarine Products Ltd*)	53
Twin-cylinder manifold (*Submarine Products Ltd*)	53
Atlantic demand valve (*Submarine Products Ltd*)	53
Two-piece dry frogman suit	54
Heavy duty frogman suit	54
Constant volume suit	71
Oil proof standard dress and corselet	71
Tucking inner collar into six-bolt corselet (*author*)	72
Deep sea leads for standard diver (*author*)	72
Control panel for one standard diver (*author*)	89
Cressi oxygen rebreather (*author*)	89
Standard diver boots	90
Divers' knives	90
Helmet and twelve-bolt corselet	107
Two-diver mobile compressor unit	107
Twin-cylinder handpump	108

Illustrations

HP reducing valve	page 108
Standard diver telephone for two divers	125
Portable compressor unit (*Midland Diving Equipment Ltd*)	125
Submersible decompression chamber	126
SDC and recompression chamber	126
Capillary type depth gauge	143
Sealed beam underwater lamp	143
Oxy-hydrogen underwater cutting torch	144
Types of exploders (*ICI*)	144

(*All pictures not otherwise acknowledged are reproduced by kind permission of Messrs Siebe Gorman & Company Ltd*)

IN TEXT

The standard diver	*Frontispiece*
The ear	16
Depth pressures	21
International code flag 'A'	50
Six-bolt standard diving helmet	60
Outlet valves	68
Air hose	68
Inlet valve	69
Filling the cylinder	78
Decompression surface supply	82
Inserting new cuff	97
Crustacea	105
Underwater game fish	110–12
Larger fish	114
Skate and ray	116
Common sea weeds	120–2
Underwater cutting apparatus	135
Arc welding torch	137
Attaching detonator and safety fuse to cartridge	141

Illustrations

Joints used with Cordtex	page 146
Methods of preparing primer cartridge with Cordtex	148
Initiation of wet Cordtex	149
Electric fuse-head	150
Standard electric detonator and delay detonator	151
The magnetic compass	162
Rise and fall of tides	166
Cross bearings and transit bearings	168
Rope	169
Bends and hitches	171
Moorings	172
The creep	173
Mouth-to-mouth methods of resuscitation	176–7

(*All line illustrations drawn by John Horsley*)

1

THE MAN-FISH

THE seas that lap our shore are not merely the windswept heaving waste that they appear to be, but the gateway to a wonderful world in which nature has distributed by far the greater proportion of living miracles. Having once penetrated this surface barrier, the submarine explorer finds a world with an environment much more suited to the support of life than that of the atmospheric world above.

All surface creatures are dragged down by gravitation, blistered and frozen in turn by extremes of temperature, and blown about by tempestuous winds. Fish and marine mammals suffer far fewer climatic changes, and float through life in a delightful state of weightlessness in an ethereal element where violence is limited to meal times, and noise is an import from another world.

Due to the density of water, life in the sea moves relatively slowly, and nature, having predestined that man shall find 'truth' beyond the stars, had perforce to coax his reptilean ancestors to crawl forth from the comforts of the ocean to live in a thinner medium where life's tempo quickened and intelligence could develop. Two hundred million years later their descendants struggle to leave the atmospheric ocean, driven by the same impelling instinct into the even more hostile environment of cosmic space.

But evolution often backtracks, and creatures whose immediate ancestors lived on land, return to the sea. The seals, second only in intelligence to man, thought of submarine comforts long ago, but as nature never returns what has once been given up as useless, did not return to them their gills, and they have to manage with the lungs our common ancestors struggled to acquire.

THE SWIM-DIVER

A species of man called 'diver', as much a throwback as the seal, acquires a mechanical lung and glides back into the primitive depths whence he came. The descent subjects the human body to an increase in pressure which, although more or less unfelt, has to be considered and well understood. Having taken into account this considerable change in our environment, and having learnt to adapt ourselves to the new conditions, we can, in reasonable safety, venture into a primitive world that has seen little change over millions of years.

Man has been diving since historic times, and for several hundred years has been using various forms of breathing apparatus to extend his underwater explorations. Not unnaturally his first idea was to extend a tube from the surface down into the water, from the bottom of which one would expect to suck sufficient atmospheric air to support life. Unfortunately, the increased pressure, due to the weight of water above the diver, limits this beautifully simple apparatus to a depth of 3 or 4 ft. Beyond this depth, even a strong man cannot force his muscles to open his rib cage, which in turn expands his lungs, for the necessary inhalations.

However, the breathing tube, often called a 'snorkel', enables a man to breath when just submerged, and as the average body will float when completely immersed, the swimmer can hang motionless in a state of rest. With a moulded rubber face mask he can observe life below the surface whilst still breathing comfortably, and he only requires the addition of swimfins to his feet, with which he can more easily propel himself through the water, to equip him so that after a little practice he can very well emulate his next of kin, the seal.

The most common practice is to have a separate breathing tube with a rubber moulded mouthpiece. The mouthpiece has protrusions which are gripped lightly by the teeth, and a flange of rubber which nestles between the teeth and the lips. The tube is tucked inside the headband of the face mask, or is secured to the headband by a smaller rubber band. Some types of breathing tube are built into the face mask, and they are satisfactory provided the mask is extended over the mouth and under the chin. The type which does not cover the mouth and relies on nose breathing, is not to be recommended, as even the smallest amount of water collecting in the bottom of the mask, is sniffed up the nose. The simple breathing tube has a single bend from the mouthpiece and then extends straight up for a few inches above the head, when the skin-diver or, to coin a better name, swim-diver is in a horizontal attitude.

The swim-diver wishing to make a descent, inhales through his tube a sufficient quantity of air, making sure he does not overfill his lungs as this promotes a choking sensation, executes a surface dive, and descends to a modest depth until the need for a fresh supply of air is felt. His legs working from the hips with a much slower stroke than that used in the crawl stroke, move him at surprising speed through the water. On surfacing he exhales through his tube, which clears it of water for the next inhalation.

The upper ends of breathing tubes can be fitted with various types of automatic valve that close on descent, keeping the tube free of water. A double bend tube, even without a valve, will stay reasonably empty by virtue of the air lock formed by the top bend, but as they are prone to tangle with weed, many swim-divers prefer the more simple type.

Whilst it is true that remarkable descents are made with only atmospheric air in the lungs, descents of more than 30 ft are not to be advised, as the increasing pressure of the water acts on the body so that the original air at atmospheric pressure is reduced in volume until it is at external water pressure. As the volume decreases, positive buoyancy changes to negative buoyancy and also there comes a point at which the rib structure is subjected to unnatural stresses and injury can result. Quite apart from the limiting factor of pressure, a second danger due to hyperventilation of the lungs, must be guarded against.

From experience the underwater swimmer discovers that by overbreathing, that is, taking several long deep breaths before his descent, he can wash out much of the residual CO_2 in his lungs and body. This enables him to hold his breath for a longer period before the percentage build up of CO_2 in his blood stream stimulates the respiratory centre in his brain, which in turn forces him to inhale and replenish the oxygen supply his body needs. Carried to excess, overbreathing can be extremely dangerous, as the brain can be starved of oxygen before the build up of CO_2 reaches the percentage necessary to promote breathing, and the victim loses consciousness.

An adult pair of lungs, containing one free volume gallon of air, has enough oxygen for three minutes with the person in a state of rest. For this reason it is not wise for underwater swimmers to compete against each other in endurance or in depth of dive. It is an interesting fact that the same lungs filled with pure oxygen will sustain life for fifteen minutes.

A descent beyond 100 ft can result in the blood being squeezed into the lung air sacs, causing damage to the lungs, after which the chest walls collapse and death is immediate. Skin diving to 100 ft is not uncommon, but mainly by races of people whose families for generations have lived in and under the water. There is a recorded case of a skin-diver reaching a depth exceeding 190 ft, but he became a casualty. Swim diving by us less aquatic mortals should not be indulged in beyond 30 ft.

DIVING PHYSIOLOGY

For the human body to descend comfortably into the depths, it requires a sufficient supply of a breathable mixture at the same pressure as the water surrounding the lungs. As the body is made up of solids and fluids which, for practical purposes, are incompressible, and air spaces which can be supplied with air or oxygen at the surrounding water pressure, it can then be subjected to great pressure without suffering discomfort or damage due to pressure alone.

As the rate of change of pressure decreases with depth, equalisation of air pressure in the body is a bigger problem near the surface than it is at depth.

Important air spaces that must be kept at external water pressure, are the internal ear cavities which are connected to the throat by the eustachian tubes. These tubes are so shaped that it is difficult to transfer pressure from the throat to the internal ear cavity where it is required to balance off the pressure outside the ear drum. On descent, failure to balance off the pressure on either side of the ear drum results in pain and eventually a ruptured ear drum. On ascent, the shape of the eustachian tube is such that the excess pressure inside the ear drum can easily relieve itself by way of the throat, and divers only experience a warm bubbling sensation in the ears.

When nature provided us with our eustachian tubes, which are only the diameter of the lead in a pencil, the change of pressure the ears had to contend with was only that due to variations in barometric pressure and the ascent of hills, etc. The natural movement of our jaws and the action of swallowing allows any differential pressures between the middle ear and ambient pressure to balance off naturally.

However, the change of pressure due to descent in water, is so great that nature has to be supplemented by artificial means, and the most effective method is to exhale against a nose clip, or the face mask whilst it is being pressed up against the nostrils, or by pressing the nose hard against the corselet when using standard diving gear. When using an aqualung with a mouthpiece, the diver's mouth is open, so he must develop the trick of closing his epiglottis, otherwise he merely exhales through the mouth and the required increase of pressure, which he requires in the throat to force air through his eustachian tube to the middle ear, is not available.

When ear pain indicates to the descending diver that internal and external pressures require balancing, he halts his descent and exhales against a nose clip. An internal movement of the ear drums and the relief of pain indicate that the desired balance has been obtained. If they are obstinate, the diver must ascend a foot or two until the pain is relieved, and again exhale against his nose clip. This is often necessary as the trumpet shaped tubes are flattened by the excess pressure in the throat so that, whilst the differential pressure exists (and the pain), it is difficult for the air readily to pass through into the internal ear cavity. It is also possible to clear the eustachian tubes by swallowing, but the nose clip method is most effective with the majority of divers.

Many divers are discouraged on their first descent by the difficulty they experience in clearing their ears but, unless they suffer from catarrh, the ability comes with practice. However, it is a mistake to press on regardless of the pain, as a ruptured ear drum can easily result. A cold in the head will block the tubes with mucus and, if it cannot be cleared by the energetic use of a handkerchief, diving must be called off for the day.

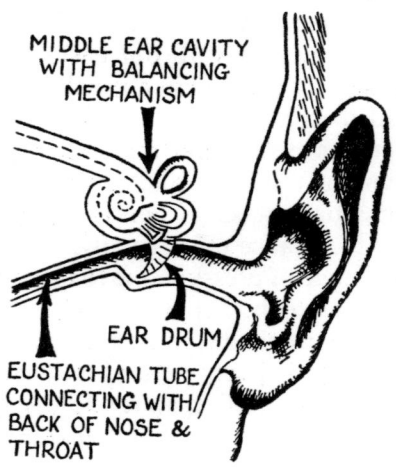

The ear

A ruptured ear drum in itself is not so serious, but temporary deafness and the danger of infecting the raw wound will restrict one's activities for some time. When using apparatus which exposes the ear drum direct to water, a ruptured ear drum allowing cold water to reach the inner ear, may cause the diver to lose all sense of balance. This could be most disconcerting underwater and, in free diving, not a little dangerous. This same vertigo and nausea may also be caused without rupturing the ear drum, if hot or cold water suddenly reaches the external ear. Divers are advised to hang on to the nearest stable object until the dizzy turn passes off, which it will do as soon as the water reaches the body temperature.

Ear plugs must on no account be used as, apart from the fact that they prevent the required equalisation of pressure on either side of the drum, they will also tend to be forced into the outer ear by external pressure. Damage to an ear which results in bleeding requires medical attention, as serious infection of the inner ear may result.

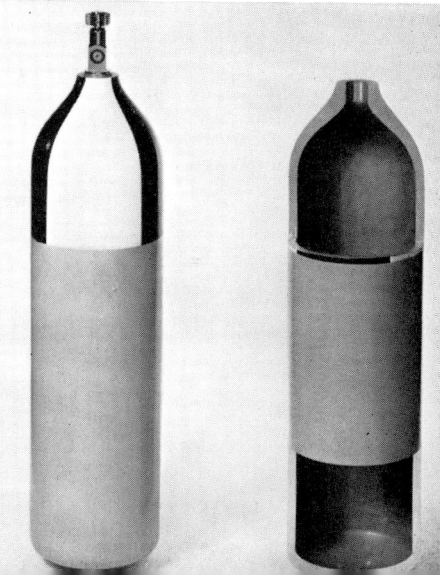

Page 17 (*above*) Twin-cylinder aqualung and dry suit; (*right*) HP alloy cylinder for use with aqualung apparatus; cut through section showing material thickness

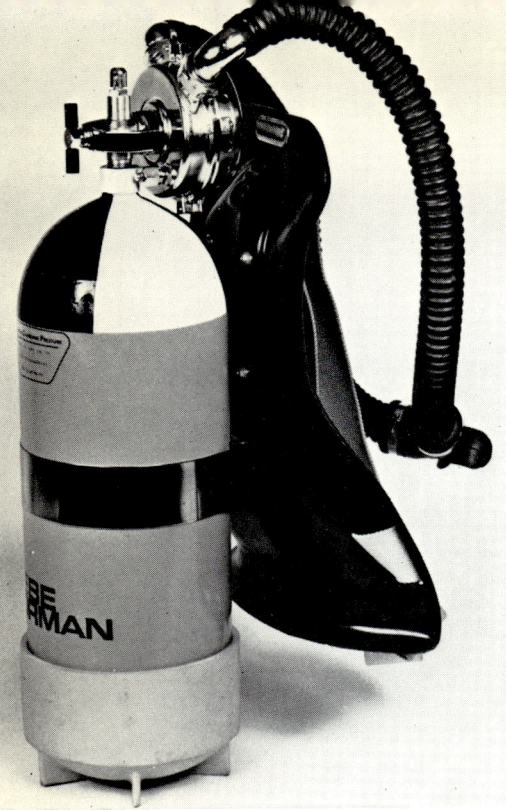

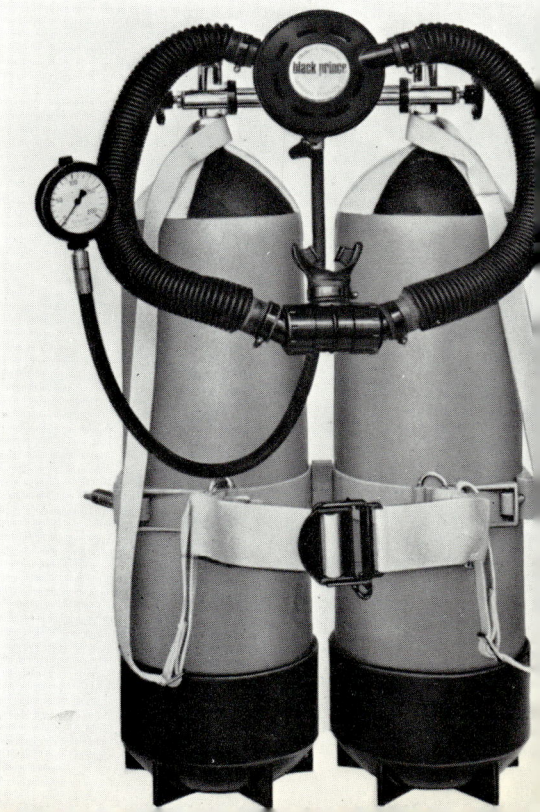

Page 18 (*above*) Single cylinder aqualung with Mistral demand valve; (*below*) Black Prince twin-cylinder aqualung

Associated with the eustachian tubes are the sinus passages which must also be clear if internal pressures are to be equalised. It is obvious, therefore, that anyone suffering from sinus trouble, is most unsuitable for diving.

When the ears are covered, as they are in a dry frogman type suit, there is a further complication which results in 'reverse ear', but this problem is dealt with in Chapter 9, Protective Clothing.

2
TO BE FOREWARNED

THERE is little in common between the breathing tube and the more ambitious compressed air or oxygen apparatus. The habits developed in skin diving, such as filling lungs for descent, and holding the breath for long periods, including ascent, are the worst possible habits to acquire when using breathing apparatus. Indeed, the holding of breath on ascent is extremely dangerous and has caused many fatalities.

After considerable skin diving, a diver in an emergency, having run out of air or having suffered mechanical failure of the apparatus, instinctively reverts to skin diving practice and fails to allow the compressed air or oxygen in his lungs to expand and escape from his mouth during the forced ascent. Failure to vent the air from the lungs will cause the lungs to overfill, air will be forced into tissue and blood vessels, and bubbles of air may reach the heart. This condition is known in the medical profession as air embolism, and apart from immediate distress, often on ascent, may be followed by partial paralysis, unconsciousness and death.

Air may also be forced into the chest cavity, outside the lungs, which during ascent expands and displaces the heart and lungs. The symptoms are shortness of breath, blueness of skin, distressed condition, etc. Only expert treatment, using a recompression chamber, can help the diver, and in the latter case, a surgical operation is required to release the trapped air. It is most important that a diver's training includes 'exhalation on ascent' exercises, especially as fear itself can cause a restriction of the throat, which will prevent natural venting. It must be an instinctive reaction, and this can only be achieved by practice. Using self-contained apparatus the diver should deliberately simulate

To Be Forewarned

air supply failure by removing his mouthpiece, and ascend up the shot rope with his lips in a whistling attitude, venting all the time, and ascending at large bubble speed. This 'free ascent' technique involves a rate of ascent in excess of the decompression speed of 25 ft a minute (speed of a 'pin head' sized bubble) and is only used in an emergency. Under training a 'free ascent' should be followed by a descent and the normal decompression ascent.

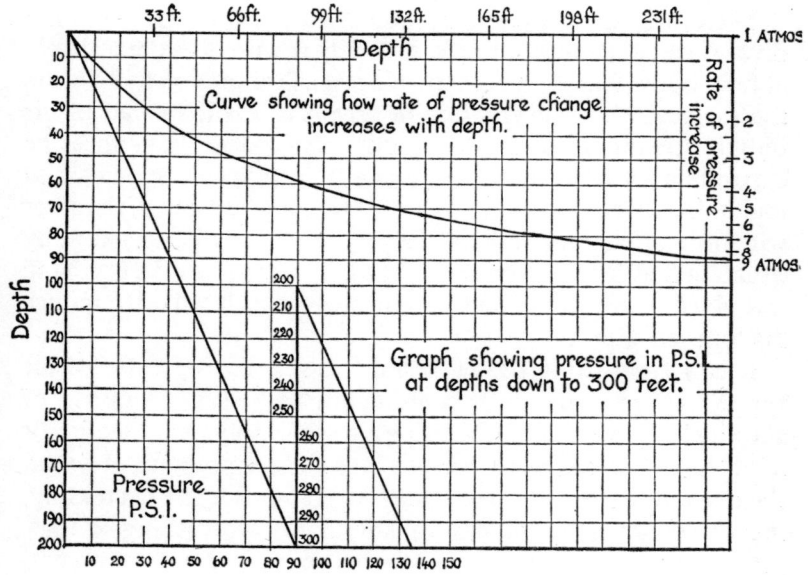

Depth pressures

Gases forming at depth in the diver's stomach will also give expansion trouble on ascent, resulting in acute pain, so large meals and gas producing foods, together with carbonated drinks, must be avoided prior to a descent.

DEPTH PRESSURES

An indication of the violent change of pressure in water is made by considering the fact that from outer space down to the earth's surface, the pressure changes from zero to 14·7 psi, in a distance of many miles. Yet in the first 33 ft of water depth, another 14·7 psi is added, giving a total pressure of 29·4 psi, or two atmospheres absolute. Continuing down to 66 ft the pressure increase is another 14·7 psi, making a total pressure of 3 atmospheres absolute. It will be seen that in the second 33 ft of water, the total pressure has only risen by 50 per cent, whereas the first 33 ft of water increased the total pressure on the diver by 100 per cent.

Therefore, as the pressure gradient flattens out with depth, a diver rising at a constant rate, will only require to exhale slowly at first, but will need to increase his rate of exhalation as he nears the surface. If the diver's rate of ascent is less than that of his bubble stream he must swim harder and exhale less, until the expanding air in his lungs has given him sufficient buoyancy to maintain free bubble speed. With his weights jettisoned, the diver will more often than not have to slow down his rate of ascent by exhaling a little faster and reducing his swimming efforts. Using less physical effort will be to his advantage as it will also reduce his 'oxygen want'.

It is a comforting thought that a diver, having suffered air supply failure at depth, is more concerned with getting rid of surplus air, than that of obtaining a fresh supply. Another factor in his favour is that as he ascends into a lesser pressure of water, the tension of the carbon dioxide (CO_2) in his lungs is decreasing, thereby diminishing the natural stimulant to breathing so that, presuming he can maintain a constant minimum rate of ascent, there is no sensation of asphyxiation.

It is now agreed by submarine experts that a man escaping from a submarine does not require any apparatus, providing he has not been subjected to pressure long enough to require stage decompression. The diver, using any type of apparatus, has to contend with this hydrostatic pressure at all times. Apart from the immediate direct effect of pressure already dealt with, there are more subtle phenomena which are none the less serious.

The most convenient gass for supplying to a diver is naturally atmospheric air, which consists of 79 per cent nitrogen, 21 per cent oxygen, together with ·03 per cent CO_2 and small amounts of argon and traces of rarer gases. Normally the nitrogen content of the air we breathe acts merely as a 'makeweight'. Oxygen is absorbed from the mixture by the blood as it passes through the lungs, and is replaced by CO_2. The increase in CO_2 has a catalytic effect which stimulates the breathing action, and the percentage of CO_2 present determines the rate of respiration.

Although small in amount, the percentage of CO_2 present is critical and a small increase over normal will result in panting and distress. It will be seen that CO_2 has an important part to play in respiration and does a useful job. It is not actually poisonous, as carbon monoxide (CO) is, and even after a diver has relapsed into unconsciousness through CO_2 contamination, he soon recovers if he is removed from the contamination in sufficient time before the brain cells are damaged or life is extinct.

THE BENDS

When breathing air under pressure, a part of the nitrogen content is absorbed into the body tissue, and whilst under a constant pressure or an increasing pressure, has no effect and causes no trouble. However, as pressure is reduced during a diver's ascent, the blood and tissue becomes saturated with nitrogen, and bubbles of the gas begin to form. The result is a condition called the 'bends' or more correctly 'compressed air illness'. A mild attack may result in a skin rash, especially if the diver is chilled, but more severe symptoms are the dull aching pains in joints, muscles and bones. An extreme attack may include asphyxia, dizziness, convulsions and paralysis. Whilst the formation of bubbles in the spinal cord will lead to paralysis of the legs, bubble formation in the blood vessels themselves may fill the right side of the heart with air, causing immediate death.

Symptoms of the 'bends' usually develop within an hour of surfacing, but they may be delayed up to twelve hours or more. As fatty tissue absorbs nitrogen more slowly than lean tissue, it follows that, everything else being equal, a fat person is less suitable as a diver than a lean person. Also, an unfit diver is more susceptible to nitrogen absorptions than his healthy counterpart. An excess of CO_2 will also aggravate the onset of the bends.

To counteract this dangerous formation of bubbles in the divers' system, it is necessary to ascend to a lower pressure slowly enough to allow the excess nitrogen to be carried away harmlessly by the bloodstream, eventually to be exhaled from the lungs as a gas.

Luckily, 'blood being thicker than water', bubbles do not form so readily as they would in water, making possible the practice of stage decompression. As the blood can hold in solution approximately twice the amount of nitrogen, at any given pressure, as water, it is safe to ascend from any pressure depth to half that pressure depth without the danger of bubble formation.

When compiling decompression tables, this rule can be applied for moderate depths, but for deep diving the ratio is reduced. It is therefore possible for a diver to ascend from a depth of less than two atmospheres (33 ft) to the surface, without any stage decompression, regardless of the duration of the descent. Ascending from greater depths, it is safe to ascend, say, from six atmospheres (165 ft) to three atmospheres (66 ft) reasonably quickly, and then desaturate by stages at predetermined depths, for periods of time based on the total duration of the descent. If blood had the same properties as water, then stage decompression could not be used, and the diver would have to decompress by means of a very slow continuous ascent, which would be almost impossible to control.

It has been proved that exercise by the diver during decompression has an adverse effect, contrary to the theory held by some diving authorities.

It will be seen from the decompression tables that the stages lengthen as the diver approaches the surface. To reduce the long tedious waiting periods on the shot rope, pure oxygen can be fed to the diver at depths not exceeding 33 ft or, when using a submerged decompression chamber, from depths of 60 ft. The reason for this is that oxygen under pressure has less poisonous effect when the diver is surrounded by air instead of water, as he is in a submerged decompression chamber. However, these facilities are usually only available to the naval diver and deep sea salvage contractors.

When oxygen is used to reduce the decompression periods,

the period given in the tables for atmospheric air is divided by 2·5. Thus a decompression stage requiring ten minutes on atmospheric air, can be reduced to four minutes when breathing pure oxygen.

If repetitive deep descents are made within a twelve-hour period, the sum of the durations of all descents and the deepest descent, are used for entering the decompression tables. If available, the *US Navy Repetitive Dive Tables* can be used with advantage, as they allow a credit for the time on the surface between descents. Only one descent exceeding 180 ft should be made within a period of twenty-four hours. When the diver's depth does not coincide with a tabulated depth, select the next deeper tabulated depth for decompression purposes. The diver's ascent should never exceed a rate of 25 ft per minute, and the time taken to ascend from the 10 ft stage to the surface should not be less than one minute.

If, from any reason, a diver is forced to omit any stage decompression required for the depth and duration of his descent, he must be sent down again as soon as possible to carry out the required decompression. Using standard diving apparatus, even an unconscious diver can be lowered gently to the required depth with his outlet valve wide open. Using self-contained apparatus, this 'cruel to be kind' treatment is not practical. The patient must then be moved to the nearest recompression chamber, which might be a naval dockyard. With the best will in the world, the local hospital can do little to help a victim of compressed air illness.

In an emergency, with no expert recompression facilities available, service tables allow the victim to be lowered to 100 ft, or the maximum depth available if less, for five minutes, after which the diver is brought up at the following rates:

From 100 ft to 70 ft at 2 ft in 3 minutes
    70 ft to 35 ft at 2 ft in 5 minutes
    35 ft to 0 ft at 2 ft in 8 minutes

Diving physiology and the theory of decompression is an inexact science due to the varying tolerances and resistances offered in the metabolism of the human body. On the other hand recompression carried out without experience and a certain amount of knowledge, could result in the victim absorbing more nitrogen into the tissues and becoming a worse case of compressed air illness as a result of the longer period under pressure. Expert medical supervision is therefore desirable and can normally be obtained at some naval dockyards.

It is possible to relieve the painful effect of the 'bends' with nicotinic acid (C_5H_4N COOH), and many cases that have failed to respond to recompression have enjoyed a dramatic alleviation of the joint pains. Dr Peter Jones decided that the actual pains were related to the spasm of the small blood vessels (arterioles) and that the symptoms were therefore likely to be relieved by some vasodilating agent, and nicotinic acid appeared a suitable preparation.

The usual method of treatment is to give slowly by the intravenous route 100 mg of nicotinic acid, taking about two minutes for the injection. This produces in most cases a tingling sensation in the hands and feet, with immediate relief of pain. The injection can be repeated in an hour with perfect safety if the first injection proves insufficient, as the drug is fairly rapidly destroyed in the body, although the effect is lasting.

Nicotinic acid can be obtained in tablet form but, as yet, they have not been used in treating the 'bends'. However, when given for other conditions, they sometimes produce the same tingling sensation in the limbs, so it is likely that 100 mg tablets will also give relief, but not so quickly.

NITROGEN NARCOSIS

The partial pressure of nitrogen in atmospheric air is responsible for a phenomenon known as nitrogen narcosis. Its effect varies with different people, being more pronounced with imaginative, excitable or neurotic types. The symptoms are generally those of intoxication and serious mental aberration. The conditions can, to some extent, be controlled by will power, and considerable deep diving experience reduces the tendency to lose command of the situation.

Nitrogen narcosis can be expected to reduce the efficiency of the inexperienced diver from 150 ft onwards, and his reaction may be the same as for alcoholic intoxication or oxygen starvation. Any apparatus allowing a concentration of CO_2 to build up, or the accumulation of CO_2 in the body due to heavy exercise, will aggravate the condition. An immediate ascent to a lesser pressure will return to the diver his normal faculties.

The use of helium instead of nitrogen in the breathing mixture entirely eliminates the dangerous narcosis, but helium, outside the Americas, is a very rare gas and the expense rules it out for small diving operations. The Americans are lucky in having the world's only known supply in quantities that are of any commercial use. The use of helium does not lessen the need for stage decompression. The ratio of the pressure of nitrogen in the diver's body to the external pressure can be 2:1, as mentioned earlier, before bubble formation can commence, but with helium the ratio is only 1·7:1. This necessitates the first stage decompression stop to be carried out lower when using helium, than when using nitrogen. As helium is a very good conductor of heat, it is necessary to have electrically heated diving dresses when working in sea temperatures below 60 degrees.

Hydrogen has similar virtues to helium in that a diver remains clear headed and efficient at depths exceeding 150 ft. It is in plentiful supply but, unfortunately, in certain proportions, oxygen and hydrogen will explode spontaneously. For use as a safe breathing mixture, it is necessary to vary the proportional ratios with changes of depth. Experiments have been made in the past and, no doubt, will be made in the future, using hydrogen and oxygen mixtures, but it is not a mixture for the uninitiated to experiment with.

OXYGEN POISONING

It comes as a surprise to most people interesting themselves in underwater swimming and diving for the first time, to learn that oxygen—the very breath of life—becomes poisonous under pressure, or as a partial pressure when mixed with other gases, of two atmospheres or more. This limits its use to a depth of 33 ft. The safe period is further reduced by heavy exertion, and even in water less than 33 ft deep the diver may suffer from oxygen blackout.

It is a fact that no two people have the same resistance to

oxygen poisoning, and that any one person's resistance varies from day to day. The first symptoms of oxygen poisoning may be a trembling of the lips, tremor, tingling of the body and/or the twitching of muscles. The immediate action is to ascend to a safe depth at once, when no harm will result, but failure to recognise the warning will certainly result in convulsions. Some divers seem to receive no prior warning, but just lose consciousness.

As the oxygen content of atmospheric air is roughly a fifth, it is obvious that having descended to a pressure of ten atmospheres (approximately 300 ft), the partial pressure of the oxygen will be two atmospheres. So that as 33 ft is the safe limit breathing pure oxygen, 300 ft is the safe limit when breathing atmospheric air. Several divers using self-contained apparatus have ignored this fact with fatal results.

Descents beyond the ten atmosphere pressure level are only made when using a breathing mixture containing a smaller proportion of oxygen, depending on the working depth. On the other hand, man cannot survive for more than a few minutes without a sufficient supply of oxygen. A shortage of oxygen over a short period will result in anoxia or 'oxygen lack' and permanent damage to the brain. The minimum oxygen requirement is 20 per cent at surface pressure; 16 per cent will result in muscular weakness and giddiness, and 14 per cent may well result in fainting fits.

CARBON DIOXIDE CONTAMINATION

The amount of carbon dioxide (CO_2) involved in respiration, although relatively small, is extremely critical. Atmospheric air contains ·03 per cent CO_2. When this is increased to 3 per cent, a rapid increase of breathing results. A further increase to 6 per cent will cause distress and over 10 per cent extreme distress, followed by unconsciousness and death at approximately 20 per cent.

Every gas in a mixture of gases has its own partial pressure, so that as the total pressure increases, the partial pressure of each gas will rise in proportion. The ill effects of a poisonous gas in a mixture of gases are increased when under pressure, and the effect of a certain percentage of CO_2 in a mixture can be ascertained by multiplying the percentage at atmospheric pressure by the absolute pressure. From this it will be seen that an acceptable 1 per cent on the surface will cause panting at 66 ft (3×1 per cent), and 3 per cent at the surface would cause great distress at 66 ft and unconsciousness at 132 ft.

It is most important, therefore, that self-contained breathing apparatus is designed with CO_2 contamination in mind, and that the air supply in diving helmets should be sufficient to ventilate efficiently. Some authorities state that the breathing of pure oxygen is quite safe in depths less than 33 ft, but this is only true when the apparatus has been very carefully designed so that there is no possibility of CO_2 build up.

The natural warning of CO_2 contamination is dizziness, fatigue, panting and nausea. The mouth and lips of a victim turn blue, and unconsciousness and death will follow. A casualty should have his air supply increased, and should be brought to the surface as soon as possible and given artificial respiration and pure oxygen if possible.

Carbon dioxide is not a poisonous gas, but it will not support life. A small excess will accelerate the onset of nitrogen narcosis, oxygen poisoning, and is the most likely cause of oxygen blackout in shallow water. As the CO_2 builds up in the lungs, the respiratory nerve centre increases the rate of breathing in order to ventilate the lungs, but when pure oxygen is being breathed, this natural reaction does not take place, the normal warning of panting does not occur, and the diver blacks out without warning.

CARBON MONOXIDE POISONING

Carbon monoxide (CO), on the other hand, is very poisonous although it is not normally present in atmospheric air. However, being a product of combustion, it is present in the exhaust gases of an internal combustion engine, and if these are allowed to reach the intake of an air compressor and are then fed to a diver, it can be very serious indeed. All exhaust gases should be led down wind well clear of the compressor. Conditions of no wind can be troublesome as the foul, contaminated air hangs around persistently, and whilst it is merely unpleasant at atmospheric pressure, being well diluted, the ill effects are magnified when breathed under pressure.

It is possible for high-pressure oil-lubricated compressors to supply for self-contained apparatus air which is contaminated by CO. This occurs if the compressor is allowed to run above its rated capacity, so that the temperature rises above the flash point of the lubricating oil This problem is dealt with in Chapter 7.

The symptoms of CO poisoning are similar to those of CO_2 contamination, but the mouth and lips turn bright red. In both cases pure oxygen should be administered and medical attention obtained. Hospitalisation and blood transfusion may well be necessary.

3
THE MEANS

BREATHING APPARATUS

THERE are three basic types of breathing apparatus available for use underwater. There is the self-contained compressed air apparatus, such as the well proven aqualung types. The spreading of underwater sport throughout the world has justified much experimentation in this type of apparatus, which, no doubt, will become even better in the future.

The second type comprises oxygen rebreathing apparatus, together with oxygen-nitrogen apparatus, the latter being most unsuitable for general use. Many expensive forms of rebreathing, or closed circuit apparatus were developed by Messrs Siebe, Gorman and by Dunlop for operational use during the Second World War, but their expense limits their use to the Services or large operators.

The third class comprises the traditional helmet type of diving gear using a surface supply of air and generally known as standard diving gear, and made in slightly different patterns by Siebe, Gorman & Co Ltd and C. E. Heinke & Co Ltd. Both firms manufactured the Admiralty Pattern, which is more or less identical, with much of the apparatus interchangeable. They also manufactured their own particular types of apparatus. C. E. Heinke & Co Ltd, developed a light-weight type of standard diving gear. Messrs Siebe, Gorman & Co Ltd, have now taken over C. E. Heinke & Co Ltd, and manufacture apparatus labelled Siebe-Heinke.

There are also sub-divisions and variations of the above apparatus, such as the demand valve surface supply apparatus.

This equipment has not the same freedom as the self-contained gear, but has an advantage in simplicity and air economy over the heavy standard gear with its extravagant air supply.

COMPRESSED AIR APPARATUS

Undoubtedly the most practical, economical and safe apparatus is based on the demand valve compressed air principle. It is not so comfortable in use as standard diving gear, at least in home waters, but most divers experienced equally in the three basic types, would use it for short duration, medium depth (100 ft) work, especially if the situation was a tricky one such as strong current, heavy traffic or when having to operate with untrained surface attendants. The author has satisfactorily completed heavy underwater concreting, for which type of work most divers would choose standard gear, using self-contained apparatus.

For all forms of underwater sport, exploration, search, etc, compressed air apparatus reigns supreme, and it has many advantages when placing charges of underwater explosives. The free-diver can be in and out of the water alternatively, placing fresh charges as fast as they can be fired.

For amateur use its advantages in safety, economy and mobility easily outpoint surface supply and oxygen rebreathing apparatus. It is nearly a hundred per cent safe, but it can only be as safe as the person using it. Well designed, it has the advantage of little or no CO_2 build up, and it can be used to considerable depths. In fact its use, in one form or another, is only limited by the breathing mixture compressed into the cylinders and by the experience of the diver.

Typical British compressed air apparatus consists of one or more cylinders containing atmospheric air compressed to 2,000 psi or more, depending on the specification to which the cylinder is manufactured. These cylinders are made from cold-drawn seamless NCM steel, heat treated and hydrostatically tested to 2,700 psi. The cylinder or cylinders are painted externally to conform with Table 1 of BSS 1319: 1946, Amendment No 1, 23.6.53, which relates to identification colours for respirable gas cylinders. They should not be painted any other colour, although a bright orange or yellow would show up much better in the water and these colours are acceptable in the US.

In Britain the Gas Cylinder (Conveyance) Regulations 1931 govern the use of high-pressure cylinders, but only whilst being carried on the public highway. They lay down the specification of the steel of which the cylinders are made, the colour of the cylinder for the gas it is to contain, the hydraulic test procedure, and the working pressure, etc.

The colour identification for compressed air is grey. The law lays down that any person or firm filling a cylinder must have carried out the hydraulic stretch test themselves within the preceding four years. In actual practice the cylinder manufacturers certificate or one issued by a firm like British Oxygen Ltd is the nearest a private owner, having his own compressor, can meet the requirement of the law. Cylinders that, when filled with water, increase their weight by less than twelve pounds, are exempt, which lets out oxygen rebreathing apparatus.

Different regulations will be found in other countries. In America the regulations are likely to vary from state to state.

In early types the air passes from the cylinder, through a control valve to a reducing valve, which reduces the pressure to around 50 psi, depending on the particular apparatus. As the diaphragm of the reducing valve is open to water pressure, or air at water pressure, the 50 psi is maintained at all depths. This low pressure air then passes to the breathing chamber, the rubber diaphragm of which is again open to water pressure on one side. On inhaling, a partial vacuum is created in the breathing chamber, the valve holding back the low pressure air is opened by the inward movement of the rubber diaphragm, and air flows into the breathing chamber.

A non-return valve on the outlet of the exhaling tube, being at the same depth and therefore at the same pressure as the rubber diaphragm, ensures that the increasing water pressure, due to descent, on one side of the diaphragm is balanced by the increasing pressure of air in the breathing chamber. Thus for any depth of water the breathing effort remains constant. Having the outlet valve in the same water pressure as the rubber diaphragm, ensures that no variation of breathing effort results from a change of attitude. If the outlet valve is at a distance of 6 in from the rubber diaphragm, the diver would find it difficult to breathe when he was in such an attitude that the valve was below and in a greater pressure than the demand valve, and when in a position with the valve above the demand valve, air rushes to waste.

The apparatus is worn on the back with the demand valve level with the shoulders, or just a little lower. The position is most important for breathing comfort. The inhaling and exhaling tubes leave the demand valve and pass, one over each shoulder, and meet at the rubber mouthpiece. A contents gauge, calibrated in pressure, completes the equipment and it is worn on the chest where it can best be seen.

The operation of the aqualung is entirely automatic, but one model of the Heinke range and the CABA had an additional emergency by-pass valve which was hand operated, and passed air straight from the cylinder to the mouth-piece. Later type demand valves now employ the single stage principle, and to improve the varying breathing characteristics of this apparatus, a small venturi tube is used to direct the air from the diaphragm controlled valve straight into the outlet port, instead of into the breathing chamber. This rush of air into the outlet port sucks air from the breathing chamber, drawing down the diaphragm, and so maintaining a flow of air with little or no effort on the part of the diver.

Foreign makes of aqualung have a reserve supply instead of the contents gauge, but the gauge is of infinitely more value when used correctly. The aqualung is a well tried and tested instrument and rarely gives trouble, and then only of a minor and unimportant nature.

A steady leak of air past the final valve can sometimes be cured by inserting the blunt end of a pencil through one of the exhaling series of holes in the demand valve cover. The rubber diaphragm can then be depressed and the rush of air will clear the valve seat of any foreign matter. If the leak persists the sintered bronze filter, which can be seen inside the cylinder clamping yoke, can be removed with the finger tip or a small screwdriver, exposing the valve spring and the valve. The nylon valve seat can then be reground very carefully on a fine flat carborundum stone or similar, or by skimming up in a lathe. If available it is better, of course, to fit a new valve.

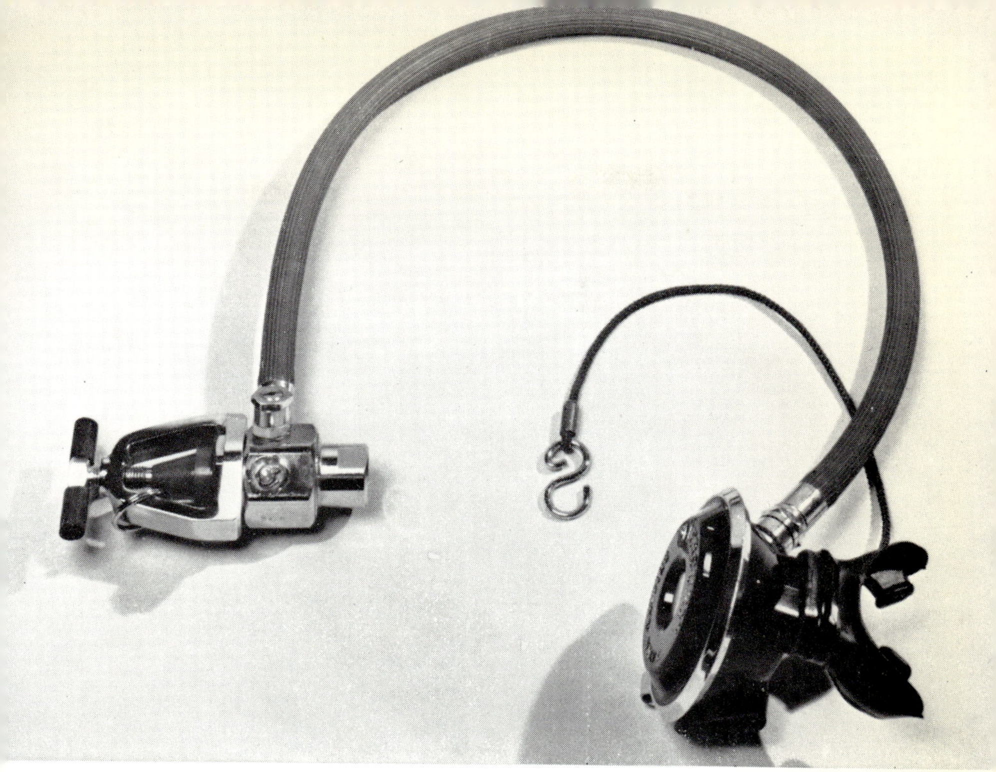

Page 35 (*above*) Mercury 2, single hose reducer and demand valve; (*below*) Merlin Mk VI demand valve

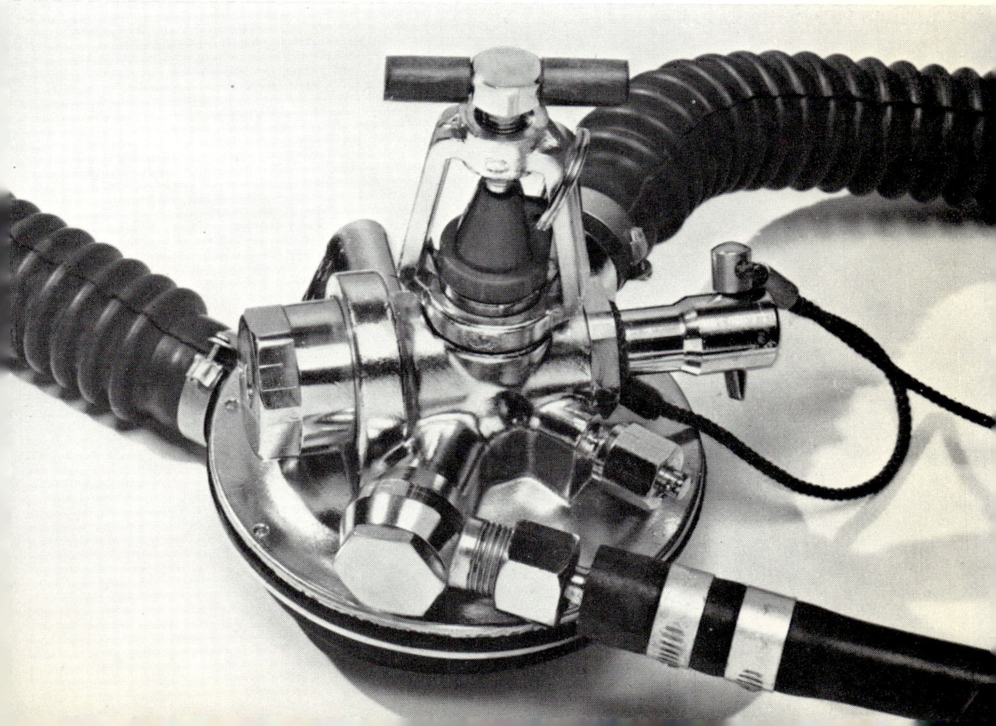

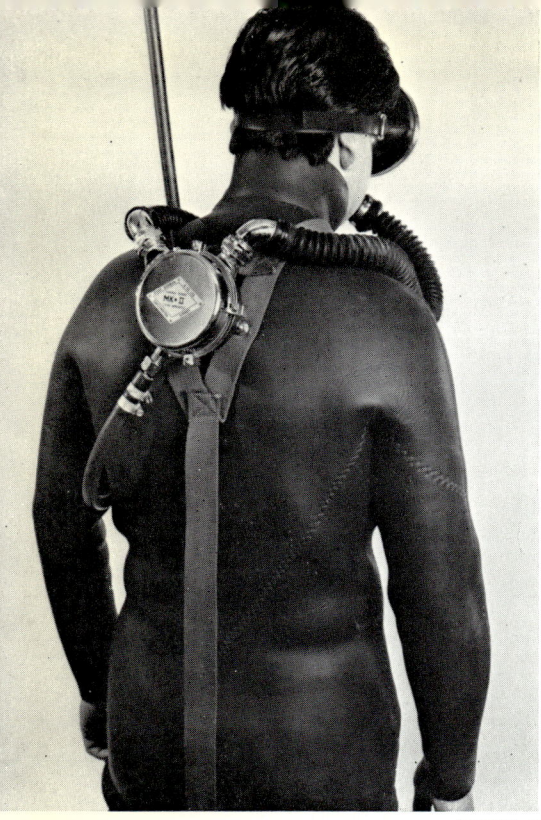

Page 36 (*above*) Mistral demand valve used for surface supply; (*below*) Mercury demand valve used with surface supply, diver wearing wet suit

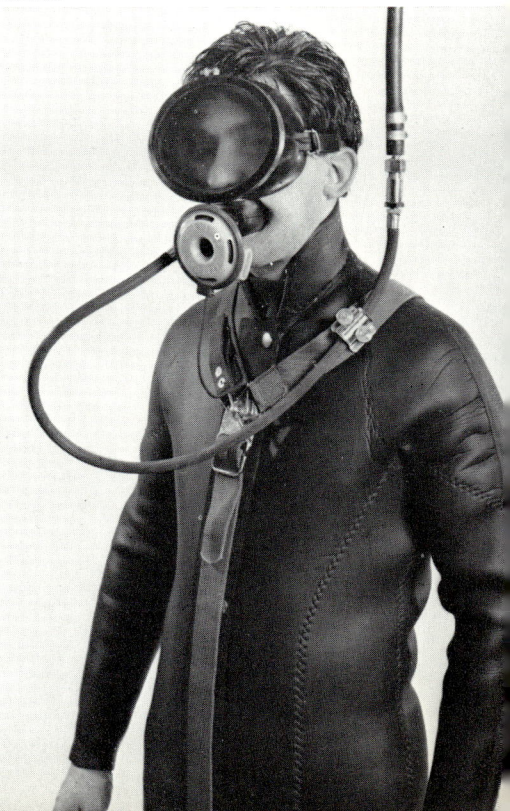

The Means

The diaphragm cover can be removed by unscrewing the clips. Inside the cover will be found the exhaling 'spear' valve. This rubber valve is bound on to a metal spigot, and sometimes a low pressure leak is experienced due to the joint not being tight. Remaking the joint with a sealing compound and rebinding securely will usually cure the trouble.

Underneath the diaphragm will be found two levers which operate a small push rod, which in turn forces the valve off its seat when the diaphragm moves inwards. If breathing becomes difficult, the levers probably require setting. The tip of the uppermost lever should be approximately $\frac{1}{4}$ in higher than a straight edge placed across the breathing chamber case. The adjustment is made by slacking off the locking nut and rotating the knurled wheel.

To test equipment, never suck directly from the outlet port of a demand valve fitted with a venturi tube, for it can happen that the servo effect is so great that the diaphragm is held fully down, and the resulting blast of air into the lungs could be fatal. The accident is not possible when the breathing tubes are fitted and air is taken from the mouthpiece in the normal manner, as the rush of air can then bypass the mouth of the user, and expend itself through the outlet 'spear' valve. If the demand valve becomes flooded with salt water, rinse out the breathing chamber with fresh water, shake out and allow to dry.

Treat the cylinders with care, as each one is a potential bomb. They are quite safe in normal use, but dropping one on to a sharp pointed object might cause a serious explosion. To avoid weakening by corrosion, rusty patches should be rubbed down lightly and touched up with grey paint.

As no foreign matter can ever get into a pressurised cylinder it is important to store them full or nearly full. Keeping the steel under tension will also retain a maximum of elasticity in the steel. When not in regular use, a breath or so of air taken every four weeks will keep the demand valve in good working order.

A single cylinder set is the most pleasant to use, having less drag in the water, less buoyancy, and therefore less lead ballast to be carried round out of the water. Positive buoyancy has to be neutralised by attaching lead ballast weights around the diver's waist.

A multi-cylinder set seems attractive ashore, or on a first class diving boat, complete with well designed ladders and platforms, but it is not so much fun in a wildly pitching boat of large dinghy size, which is the best that can often be obtained. If it is a matter of underwater endurance, then multi-cylinders are a necessary evil.

The underwater sportsman is sometimes advised to dive with a companion, also using breathing apparatus. The term 'buddy diving', of American origin, describes this method, but in the thicker tidal waters found around Britain, and in many other parts of the world, it is only false security. It is the author's experience that free-divers find it difficult and sometimes impossible to keep in visual contact, and even in clear water, unless the divers face each other, there must be a 'tail end Charlie' not being watched.

It is also a fact that when a free-diver gets into trouble, he makes straight for the surface, and that is where he requires a safety companion—in a boat preferably, or if not, with a reserve of buoyancy such as a lifebuoy, float, etc sufficient to support them both.

The case of a free-diver being trapped may be cited, but with over two thousand qualified divers, both amateur and professional, diving at sea, in harbour and docks, throughout the whole year, the British Underwater Centre has never had a case of a free-diver being trapped, and the BUC is the oldest organisation concerned with free-diving in Britain. In any case, it could only happen if a heavy body, such as a wreck, happened to move and pinned the diver down, for in any other case he could extricate himself, even if it meant removing his apparatus and making a 'free ascent'.

Again, many free-divers find it necessary to make descents when only one set of breathing apparatus is available, so it would appear to be much more sensible to practice the British method, based on individual self-reliance, from the very beginning, and not count on help from a submerged companion who may not be available when required.

A good CO_2 lifejacket is essential, as it will guide you to the surface in an emergency when diving in 'black' water, maintain your buoyancy during a 'free ascent', and will support you on the surface until the diving boat can pick you up. At 99 ft (4 atmospheres) the lifejacket will only be one quarter inflated, at 66 ft (3 atmospheres) one third, and at 33 ft (2 atmospheres) only half inflated, so such an ascent would not be as rapid as one would at first imagine. However, providing the diver has a neutral buoyancy at his working depth, operation of the CO_2 lifejacket is bound to change the buoyancy to a positive one, ensuring an ascent to the surface even if the diver loses consciousness.

If the very worst happens, it is a comfort to know that consciousness is not lost immediately water is inhaled. A free-diver should make up his mind—so that it is almost instinctive—that he will inflate his lifejacket and jettison his weights, if it is the last thing he ever does. A little trouble on the surface may prompt the diver to attempt to inflate the lifejacket manually, but this is a mistake as the situation may worsen before full inflation is achieved, and operation of the CO_2 cylinder would then burst the lifejacket.

Do not attempt to rig a ladder over the side of a small boat, but hang it over the transom (square stern) with the ladder lashed securely to thwart (seat across the boat). If no ladder is available, a bight, or loop, of line can be hung over the stern at a suitable depth so that the diver can get a foothold. It will be easier if swimfins are removed in the water.

A boat is much stiffer fore and aft than it is athwartship, and even a medium sized pram dinghy will support a diver hanging on the stern, with his assistant rowing amidship. If a diver allows himself to become exhausted, do not try to get him inboard a small boat single handed. He should hang on to the transom and allow himself to be towed to safety. A line can be passed under his arms and secured inboard if he is in a bad way.

Although compressed air apparatus is the safest and simplest of underwater breathing apparatus, it is still most desirable to receive training under a qualified instructor with all facilities laid on. However, this is not always possible, and the following stage by stage training should then be followed carefully. The exercises given are the result of much training experience and each one is included for a very good reason, however simple. They can all be repeated several times with advantage, as nothing can replace time spent underwater in building up diving experience.

4
AQUALUNG TRAINING

THE aqualung is in most common use today. The cylinder is charged with clean dry air at 2,000 psi to 3,000 psi, depending on the specification of the cylinder. The air must be free from oil droplets and vapour as the continual breathing of oil laden air is harmful. It must also be dry for, as the high pressure air is reduced in pressure, a drop in temperature occurs at the reducing valve, and there is a slight risk of freezing up the valve. Wet air will also condense in the cylinder with risk of corrosion.

APPARATUS

The demand valve yoke is threaded over the cylinder valve and the spigot nestled carefully into the groove on the cylinder valve washer. The fixing pin is registered in the conical recess at the back of the valve and tightened by hand or moderately with a spanner. If the demand valve is not square with the cylinder, do not force it round, but loosen the pin and reset.

Turn on the cylinder valve fully in an anti-clockwise direction and check pressure content of cylinder. If satisfied that there is sufficient air for the descent, turn off cylinder valve and watch pressure gauge needle. If the needle drops, there is a leak somewhere on the high pressure side of the apparatus. If leak cannot be traced by sound or feel, immerse the apparatus, keeping the mouthpiece out of the water. Bubbles will indicate the leak. Tighten up faulty connections and recheck.

To check for leaks on the low pressure side of the apparatus, suck air from the mouthpiece with the cylinder valve still in the 'off' position. If air can still be drawn from the mouthpiece when the needle on the contents gauge has dropped to zero, there is a leak on the low pressure side of the apparatus. Check corrugated tubes and connections. Turn on the cylinder valve fully and the apparatus is ready for use.

FIRST LESSON

On the first descent, dive from a boat in 15 to 20 ft of water with a companion acting as attendant. A small boat can be anchored with a warp and a 20-lb ballast weight, and this can be used as the diver's 'shot' rope. A large vessel will require to be moored and a separate 'shot' rope put down for the diver.

Adjust the shoulder straps so that the demand valve does not bang the back of the head, with the head thrown back. With the attendant holding the lung, pass the left arm through the shoulder strap, keeping the right arm free for steadying purposes in a heaving boat. Then with the left arm free, pass the right arm through the shoulder strap. Do not allow yourself to be caught with both arms trapped back in the harness, as you will fall about in a heaving boat, probably damaging yourself and equipment in the process, and most likely finish up by overturning a small boat, or pitching over the gunwale into the sea from a larger one.

Adjust the jock strap, which is passed between the legs, so that it holds the buoyant cylinder well down on the back. Do not worry about jettisoning the apparatus. It is buoyant and will help to support you on the surface. Secure the pressure gauge in a readable position and then attach the quick release, weighted belt, or lead ballast, so that it can be jettisoned in an emergency. The knife should be worn at the side or at the back, but never at the front, unless the sheath is of metal, as a diver, doubling over, has been known to drive the point of the knife clean through a leather sheath, through a light-weight suit and into his thigh.

At this stage it is wise thoroughly to clear the nose and head. The nose clip is then placed on the nose with the loop of the spring passing across the bridge of the nose. The nose clip is a most essential and desirable piece of equipment. Most divers find it quicker to clear their eustachian tubes by exhaling against a nose clip, rather than by swallowing. Also, in the event of filling or losing the face mask underwater (and it can happen so easily), two quite unnecessary holes are 'stopped' off. It is also an aid to emptying the mask underwater, as it acts as a one-way valve, and it also prevents fogging of the mask.

When using a nose clip, it is possible to suffer a minor face squeeze, due to the fact that the air in the mask starts off at atmospheric pressure. On descending, the external pressure collapses the rubber to a certain extent, after which the eyeballs tend to be sucked out of the head. It is only necessary to exhale through the nose sufficiently hard to overcome the spring tension of the clip to balance off the pressure again. With the nose clip in position, practice exhaling gently against the spring pressure until the ear drums 'move'. Do not do it violently, as the nose may start bleeding. If the ear drums do not 'move', it is unlikely that they will clear on descent.

There are many types and shapes of face mask; choose one that fits nicely. If it can be held firmly on to the face by suction alone, by inhaling through the nose, it will not leak in use.

Before fitting the mask, rub a little saliva over the inside glass and rinse out in sea-water. Shake out surplus water and fit securely to face. This treatment will help to prevent misting up. Never plunge or dive into water when wearing a face mask. Never put anything into the ears with the object of keeping the water out, as the increasing pressure of water will ram the plug into the outer ear. In any case the water pressure is required in the ears to balance off the internal pressure.

Make a light safety line fast to the upper left arm, if right-handed, with a clove hitch and a half hitch, so that it may be released easily in an emergency.

The mouthpiece is now fitted, with the rubber flange between the lips and the teeth, and the rubber nodules are held lightly between the teeth. Mould the lips around the mouthpiece, making sure that the corners of the mouth do not slacken on exhalation. Take a few light and heavy breaths to assure oneself that the air supply is available as desired.

With the attendant paying out the safety line, descend the ladder until submerged. Hand signals can be used as for standard diving (see page 65). Holding the ladder lightly, exhale. If a diver sinks slowly his ballast weight is correct. Inhaling deeply should arrest the descent. It is much better to ballast a little heavy rather than a little light. A grossly overloaded diver can swim to the surface, although he will find it difficult to stay there, but it is exhausting and sometimes impossible to swim down with too little ballast.

However, on the first descent the diver should not worry about swimming and does not wear swinfins, but takes hold of the shot rope and descends hand over hand. After descending about ten feet, most divers, on their first descent, suffer ear pain in one or both ears. The pain can be acute and it is important not to continue the descent, as a ruptured ear drum will result. Ascend a foot or two until the pain ceases, and then exhale against the nose clip. If the ears clear the descent can be continued until pain recurs. If the ears cannot be cleared, stay at a depth at which they do not hurt, and they will probably clear themselves after a few minutes.

It may be that the diver has not developed the knack of closing his epiglottis, and when he tries to exhale against his nose clip or mask the pressure in the throat is expended through the mouth, which is open when using a mouth piece. Practice clearing ears with the mouth open. If difficulty is still experienced, try the natural, but less positive, method of swallowing and moving the jaws.

It is no good trying to clear the ears whilst the pain is acute, as the eustachian tubes are flattened by the differential pressure, and air cannot be readily passed through to obtain the desired balance. If they cannot be cleared, return to the surface and try again another day. But having cleared them successfully continue to the bottom, have a look around, sit down, lie down, and take things very quietly. A nervous person will find this most difficult, and will have an overpowering desire to keep on the move, breathing more heavily with every breath until he convinces himself that the air supply is failing.

Develop the habit of checking the pressure gauge at regular intervals, or when any unusual sound becomes apparent. If the pressure gauge pipe or the gauge itself failed, air would bubble forth and the gauge would probably show a drop in pressure. As there is a restrictive device at the high pressure chamber outlet, the air supply would only bubble away to waste slowly, and not with a rush as is sometimes believed.

After some little time, signal to the attendant that you are coming up, by giving the usual four pulls on the safety line. Ascend up the shot rope, breathing steadily all the time, and take about half a minute to ascend 10 ft.

Presuming that there is no ear problem, descend to the bottom again without the shot rope, and with the safety line slack, by exhaling to lose buoyancy. On reaching the bottom again move around a little and practise standing on the hands with the legs straight up. As there is a pressure change of roughly half a pound for every foot of depth, the ears may require clearing for this change of attitude. Every descent will, of course, require the clearing of eustachian tubes, but the actual clearance becomes easier with practice.

This ascent can simulate an air supply failure, so when ready to ascend, signal the attendant, remove the mouthpiece, and ascend hand over hand up the shot rope, with the mouth in a whistling attitude, allowing air to bubble out as it expands in the lungs due to an ascent into lesser pressure. This is the 'free ascent' method of reaching the surface safely, but it does not allow for decompression, the speed being that of the largest bubbles. Venting the surplus air from the lungs during this more rapid ascent, also removes some of the CO_2 so that the tension of this gas decreases rather than increases, and there is no overpowering desire to inhale. It is wise to practise this at intervals, so that the diver overcomes any fear of air supply failure, as fear itself can constrict the air passages of the throat so that, although appreciating the seriousness of air embolism, the diver could still become a victim.

If the free-diver is ever faced with an air supply failure he would perhaps not have the benefit of a shot rope but would be swimming straight up towards the light judging his speed by the largest bubbles. If through overventing too much air from the lungs, and it is very difficult, so much buoyancy was lost that the correct speed could not be maintained, then comes the moment to operate the CO_2 lifejacket, and also the 'quick release' on the weight belt if necessary.

This first lesson should satisfy the average diver for one day, especially if not wearing a protective suit. It must always be remembered that with compressed air apparatus, the diver is

Aqualung Training 45

breathing chilled air, due to the expansion of air from the high pressure cylinder. This chilled air removes a lot of internal heat with each exhalation, but the loss is not felt internally, as it would be from the external body with its sensitive nervous system. Although feeling quite comfortable in the water, a heavy fit of shivering may follow on leaving the water, indicating the surprising amount of internal heat lost. In all diving the rule is—everything in moderation.

SECOND LESSON

During the second lesson, the use of swimfins can be mastered. There is nothing difficult to learn about their use, and a poor swimmer can propel himself most effectively underwater. Keeping the legs as straight as possible but flexible, move them up and down alternately, working from the hips. A slow steady beat is most efficient. Begin with medium sized swimfins, changing to larger stiff types as the correct leg muscles are developed. There are numerous types and shapes and, unfortunately, varying degrees of quality. It is not always economic to buy the cheapest. If they chafe the feet, wear a light pair of socks underneath.

The use of swimfins complicates the descent down a ladder, but it can be done if taken quietly. Using the safety line again, practise swimming from the surface to the bottom and up again. To commence the descent, bring the head down, and then swing the legs both together up and out of the water. Follow this immediately by emptying the lungs, and giving a pull downwards with the arms, as in the breast stroke. The diver then slides effortlessly down into the depths.

On reaching the bottom he levels out, breathing normally and propelling himself with legs only. The hands are of little use when diving naked, as the power transmitted by the swimfins pushes the diver faster than the effective use of the hands. However, the hands can be useful from time to time, when moving off in a new direction, or when suffering from the drag of a protective suit and the extra lead ballast which is then required.

As an exercise only, swim around near the bottom until exhausted. When breathing becomes an effort and every breath has to be dragged from the lung—stop—do nothing, and rest in whatever position one happens to be. Breathe gently, taking a long deep breath now and again to ventilate the lungs, and then continue breathing as gently as possible. After a minute or two you will be completely recovered. Never go to the surface when exhausted, but recover on the bottom, or half way down, or just submerged, but on no account struggle to keep your head out of the water. The effort of keeping a part of the body, unsupported by water, out of the water, only increases the fatigue.

Having discovered the ability of resting and recovering energy underwater, the swim-diver receives a wonderful new conception of underwater exploration. A new world is opened up, which suddenly becomes friendly and extremely interesting. Until this moment arrives the diver is not safe off the end of a line, and if allowed to free-dive is a potential menace to himself and his companions.

PRACTICE

Waterbatics should now be practised, including forward somersaults, rolls and loops. To complete a nice loop, swim down steeply and then with plenty of speed start curving upwards, continue up and over the top of the loop and down to the bottom again. At the top of a good loop, an aqualung often suffers a fluctuation in the air supply, due to the demand valve being in a greater pressure of water than the lungs, tending to blow the mouthpiece from the lips.

Practise swimming straight up the bubble stream. It is the shortest distance to the surface, and can be a very useful guide when swim-diving in thick water. Sand in suspension and plankton, often reflect the surface light from all directions, and without the bubble stream it can be difficult to determine which is up or down. Plankton fog can be bad in the spring and spring tides always stir up the mud and sand. In clear water the directional problem is not very great, except in azimuth, as the lighter water above allows for orientation down to 150 ft or so.

Descending in deep clear water for the first time is rather disappointing. The clear water does not reflect any light, and the watery world appears dark and forbidding down below. As the

Aqualung Training

diver approaches the bottom, the reflected light illuminates the scene as if an electric light had been switched on. This is most noticeable on a sandy bottom.

It would appear to the uninitiated that the great danger when using a separate mouthpiece is that of having it knocked or torn out of the mouth by weed, wreckage or ropes. Actually it presents no hazards whatever, and the diver should practise replacing it as often as possible. The first attempt at replacing the mouthpiece can be made at the foot of the ladder or on the shot rope. Nearly fill the lungs and remove the mouthpiece. Then, replacing the mouthpiece in the mouth carefully and without undue haste, lie over on the side so that the corrugated exhaling tube is down, and exhale into the mouthpiece. Air being lighter than water, the exhaled air will float up and fill the higher inhaling tube first, forcing the water level down the exhaling tube until both are empty. The next breath will be dry air from the demand valve. If there is a small amount of water still slopping about in the bottom tube, repeat the exhalations until the tube is quite empty. It is important to know which tube is the exhaling tube, as some models are reversed. With the exhaling tube uppermost, the air will merely go to waste and the inhaling tube will remain flooded.

In practice, the diver's lungs may be empty just when the mouthpiece is torn from his mouth. In this eventuality the mouthpiece is held up above the demand valve and the head held back with the mouth uppermost. As the demand valve is in a greater pressure than the mouthpiece, air will pour out. The mouthpiece is then brought down to the lips and the diver takes a breath of air. He can then blow the exhaling tube clear in the usual way.

A similar principle allows the face masks to be cleared of water when submerged. With the head thrown back, hold the top of the mask firmly to the forehead, and exhale through the nose by overcoming the spring pressure. This is quite easy. As air is blown into the mask, and as it cannot escape upwards, due to the pressure of the hands holding it firmly to the forehead, water, being heavier than air, is forced out of the bottom of the mask with each exhalation through the nose. If this method does not give results, the diver is most likely exhaling through the mouth unwittingly.

Having mastered free-diving to this extent, over-confidence becomes apparent, and must be guarded against. The safety line can now be dispensed with under reasonable conditions, but not the boat. With the luxury of a contents gauge, no one need ever be caught out if they practise common sense.

With a free-diver swimming steadily just beneath the surface his consumption of free-air will be, very approximately, 1 cu ft per minute. At 33 ft 2 cu ft per minute, at 66 ft 3 cu ft per minute and so on. As the amount of air required varies with depth, the amount of energy being used, the skill and experience of the diver, not to mention the different makes of breathing apparatus which can vary by 50 per cent, no one can quote accurate consumption figures.

Get in some diving hours at various depths and under varying conditions. Remember the rules and remember that whilst another diver may be able to help you when in trouble, do not rely on his help—you may be bitterly disappointed. Below the surface of the ocean a primitive but peaceful world exists—peaceful until things go wrong.

It is always easier to swim upwards than downwards. In fact it is possible to swim up with surprisingly large lumps of metal, but it is not so easy to take down even a small buoyant object. When in trouble, it is normally unnecessary to jettison the trimming ballast to reach the surface. If the boat or safety raft is not to hand when reaching the surface, the diver should get over on to his back, so that the buoyant cylinder is fully immersed, thereby giving him maximum assistance. An empty 40-cu-ft cylinder is 2 to 3 lb lighter than a full one.

Do not waste energy swimming any distance on the surface, but attract the boatman's attention and let him come to you. If a surface swim cannot be avoided, and there is any doubt about reaching security, then the jettisoning of ballast is warranted. It is a great comfort, and essential when in tidal waters, to be equipped with a CO_2 life jacket.

In smooth water the boat attendant has no difficulty in following the large bubbles of an aqualung diver in lesser depths than 50 ft. Beyond these depths the bubbles begin to break up before reaching the surface, and they are easily lost sight of. In rough water it is easy to lose sight of the large bubbles, and under these conditions the free-diver should work with a shot rope and a distance line leading from the shot.

Unless the man in the boat is an experienced seaman, it can happen that the diver leaves a fit, strong, enthusiastic attendant in the boat, but on his return to the surface, a little cold and tired himself, he only finds a shadow of a man who, prostrate with sea sickness, has long since lost all interest in his own, or the diver's safety.

If the boat attendant loses sight of the swim-diver's bubbles, in open sea conditions with little current, the boat should maintain its position and a sharp lookout should be kept for the diver on surfacing. Do not motor or row in the direction he is believed to have taken, as the odds are you will be wrong, and with the effect of wind and the speed of the boat, it is quite possible the diver will be out of sight when he does surface, except in a flat calm—and you never lose a diver under those conditions. If the boat's position is fixed, only the distance the diver can travel will separate the diver from the boat, and this is never very great.

When not using a watertight suit, a diver can enter the water safely by rolling backwards over the gunwale, holding his mask firmly on to his face until submerged. Exhaling as he enters the water will take him down well clear of the boat. A dry suited diver, if he wishes to keep dry, must make his first descent down a ladder in a dignified manner. The air having been expelled correctly, he can then roll in backwards with abandon. If he rolls in backwards with air still trapped in the suit, the air will burst out of the cuffs and hood, letting water in at the same time.

Before descending, a free diver should look around and decide whether any vessel is holding a course that might coincide with his reappearance on the surface. In any case, before surfacing, stop breathing for a moment, and listen for the sound of engines. If the volume of propeller and engine noise is increasing, stay down deep and only surface when the volume of noise is obviously diminishing. Always, on breaking the surface, look right around through 360 degrees, and be ready to dive on the instant. Even a heavy rowing boat carries a lot of weight.

At sea the flying of flags and signals must be taken seriously.

The International Code of Signals, revised in 1969, has been designed so that ships and shore stations of any nationality can easily communicate with each other. If the situation demands it, and it is considered necessary, the diving flag from the International Code of Signals is flown. This is the flag 'A', vertical white and blue with swallow tails, which indicates to the master of any vessel that you have a 'diver down'. It should not be flown at any other time, so don't be tempted to fly it as a show-off symbol—it would soon cease to be effective.

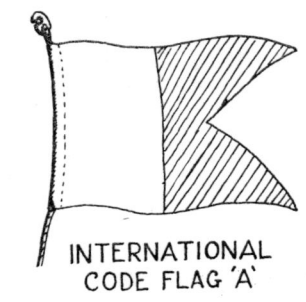

International code flag 'A'

5

OXYGEN REBREATHING APPARATUS

THERE are many variations, professional and home-made, of oxygen rebreathing apparatus. Compressed air apparatus is useless in underwater warfare as the bubble display, so valuable in normal diving, becomes a menace when an unobserved approach has to be made. Oxygen rebreathing apparatus gives off no bubbles. However, this does not help in civilian or sporting diving.

Many people condemn oxygen rebreathing apparatus out of hand, saying it is dangerous and limited in use, which is true to some extent, but a motor car, an aeroplane, and even the popular aqualung, can kill you if you use them incorrectly. As regards limited use, a tremendous amount of professional underwater work is carried out in depths of less than 33 ft, which is the maximum working depth for pure oxygen. The apparatus has the advantage of light weight and compactness, and does not depend on the availability of a high-pressure compressor. Some people believe its use is illegal in Britain. This is not so, but the 1960 Diving Special Regulations prohibit its use to employee divers, except with the special consent of a Factory Inspector. If the diver has been trained in the use of the apparatus, and the nature of the job demands it, this consent should be forthcoming. The intention of the law is to protect an employee, so that he cannot be sent down with apparatus, the dangers of which he does not understand. State regulations vary in the US.

In fact, the original draft of the proposed Diving Special Regulations also prohibited the use of compressed air apparatus, which was quite ridiculous. After consultations with the British Underwater Centre and other bodies, the regulations were amended to allow the use of aqualung apparatus.

There is no restriction whatever on the use of oxygen rebreathing apparatus by freelance working divers and sporting divers. However, for underwater sport the use of such apparatus has few advantages and some disadvantages. If oxygen is to be used, the apparatus must be well designed, and in this respect the old Mark IV Siebe Gorman Amphibian set scored all round, as it was light and convenient to wear, with the built-in safety factor of limited duration, but it is now obsolete.

APPARATUS

Oxygen rebreathing apparatus of Continental manufacture is available, such as Cressi, Pirelli and Draager, all working on the same simple principles. It is light and convenient to wear, and an entry can be made through a smaller aperture than with any other form of self-contained underwater breathing apparatus. The small capacity oxygen cylinders can be filled from any nearly full oxygen cylinder. Commercial oxygen is acceptable and can be obtained from garages, blacksmiths and engineering works.

The impurities which can occur in oxygen are traces of nitrogen and argon if the oxygen is produced by fractional distillations of liquid air, and traces of hydrogen if produced by electrolysis of water. *The British Pharmacopoeia* specifies that the supply contains not less than 98 per cent v/v oxygen and lays down stringent limit tests for CO_2, acidity, alkalinity and oxidising substances. Commercial oxygen does not legally have to comply, but in fact it is believed that there is no actual difference in quality. The extra cost is to defray the expense of testing each batch to *British Pharmacopoeia* requirements so that a legal guarantee may be given. A standard work on anaesthetics suggests that ordinary commercial oxygen be used in view of its lower cost, and categorically states that there is no risk involved.

The other requirement with oxygen rebreathing apparatus is a supply of soda lime, which is specially prepared for breathing apparatus and sold under such trade names as Protosorb, Durasorb etc. The granule size should be of 4/10 mesh, although 6/8 mesh is satisfactory. When 100 per cent oxygen is inhaled, approximately 4 per cent is absorbed by the blood and replaced

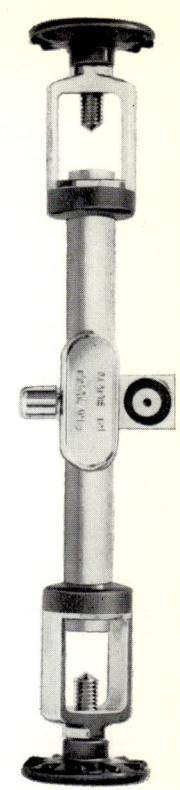

Page 53 (*above left*) Triple cylinder rig; (*above right*) twin cylinder manifold; (*below*) Atlantic demand valve

Page 54 (*left*) Two-piece dry frogman suit; (*right*) heavy duty frogman suit and surface supply demand valve apparatus

by CO_2. The soda lime absorbs the CO_2 and the oxygen consumed is replaced in the breathing bag of the apparatus from the small oxygen cylinder. Damp soda lime loses efficiency, which in turn may result in the diver suffering from a 'shallow water blackout', and a complete wetting of the absorbent can produce a caustic solution which must not be swallowed. Therefore the flooding of the apparatus from any cause whatever, should signal the termination of the dive.

Having decided to become proficient in the use of oxygen rebreathing apparatus, and already having experience with compressed air apparatus, the diver must approach his oxygen training with confidence. The apparatus will consist of a full face mask or a mouthpiece which leads via a corrugated rubber tube, through a hole in the breathing bag, to the soda lime canister. A small oxygen cylinder containing about 4 cu ft at 2,000 psi, is secured to the bottom of the breathing bag. In the Mark IV Amphibian apparatus and the more sophisticated service sets, a small reducing valve fitted with a restrictor feeds approximately 1 litre of oxygen a minute from the cylinder into the breathing bag. The flow can be adjusted to match the consumption of the particular diver, which in the case of the operational frogman is more or less constant, as he swims steadily towards the target. However, the working diver does not do much swimming, but descends down a shot rope, examines the job, works on it, rests—his consumption varying all the time. In this case the reducing valve is more trouble than it is worth, and it is preferable to work on demand, replenishing the breathing bag as required by means of a simple on/off valve such as is fitted to the Cressi and Pirelli apparatus.

Having filled the canister with soda lime and the cylinder with oxygen, the apparatus is assembled and checked for leaks by exhaling through the mouthpiece into the breathing bag until it is full. The mouthpiece valve is then turned off, and the bag squeezed to show up any possible leaks.

USE OF APPARATUS

The apparatus is now ready for use. The breathing bag is worn on the chest and secured round the neck and with a waist belt fitted with a quick release fastener. A weighted belt is required, as with an aqualung, to neutralise any positive buoyancy. With any type of apparatus utilising a breathing bag in the system, the final trim can be obtained by adding or expelling gas from the bag.

Before entering the water, the breathing bag and lungs must be emptied of all air, as no nitrogen must be present in the closed circuit. If nitrogen were left in the breathing bag and lungs, it would be possible to use the apparatus below 33 ft without the risk of oxygen poisoning, but the great danger of having nitrogen in the rebreathing apparatus is that, if oxygen supply fails or is fully consumed when working on demand, the diver is left breathing inert nitrogen which will not support life. As the CO_2 produced is absorbed by the soda lime, the diver suffers no distress or warning signs and a condition of anoxia, or oxygen starvation, results. Without any warning the diver loses consciousness, and in minutes the brain cells can be permanently damaged.

To remove nitrogen from the apparatus, collapse the breathing bag by inhaling through the mouthpiece and exhaling through the nose or through the mouthpiece, if a two way cock is fitted. Then, with the bag quite empty, flush up with pure oxygen by operating the oxygen bypass valve or cock. Inhale pure oxygen from the bag deep into the lungs, exhaling through the nose or two way mouthpiece cock, and then repeating a second time before putting on nose clip and/or mask.

Enter the water quietly and breath with deep long breaths. This is necessary so that the short single breathing tube is completely scavenged, thus eliminating the possibility of any CO_2 build up. When using oxygen rebreathing apparatus the smallest concentration of CO_2 seems to affect the diver and increases the risk of oxygen shallow water blackout, or at least will produce headaches and stuffiness. At the end of each inhalation there should be a small quantity of oxygen left in the breathing bag, and the lead ballast should be adjusted so that this is so. As oxygen is consumed, the diver's buoyancy will become negative, and it is then necessary to add oxygen to the bag, to bring it back to neutral. If the diver is too buoyant, he can let oxygen out of the breathing bag by operating the relief valve which is fitted to some models, or if not fitted, he can ex-

Oxygen Rebreathing Apparatus

hale it through the nose by overcoming the nose clip, or with a full face mask by exhaling the surplus oxygen away from slack lips around the mouthpiece.

When using oxygen apparatus, over-exertion must be avoided at all times. If any signs of panting occur, stop immediately and inhale and exhale deeply until recovered. If beyond recovery, surface immediately, exhaling on the ascent to prevent any damage to the lungs. When swimming out of trim, too buoyant or too heavy, a neutral trim may be obtained by changing depth. If you are sinking, go up a bit, and *vice versa*.

Although, by calculation, there is sufficient absorbent in the canister to use it a second time, do not be tempted to do so, as the efficiency of the soda lime falls as it is used. As a safeguard, the canister is designed to take double the amount required. An oxygen rebreathing set designed for one hour's duration will require 2 lb of soda lime—1 lb for one hour plus 100 per cent factor of safety. Recharge the canister with fresh soda lime for every refill of oxygen. Stale, doubtful, soda lime, the result of continual exposure to the atmosphere through the lid being left off, or a damaged container, should be rejected.

Some thought and careful design must go into the canister, as it must contain sufficient absorbent to cope with the production rate of CO_2, with the 100 per cent factor of safety, and it must be baffled so that the whole volume of absorbent is doing its job. With a badly designed canister, it is possible for the quantity to be sufficient, but due to a part of its volume being bypassed, the effective soda lime becomes exhausted so that a build-up of CO_2 can occur with risk of shallow water blackout. Heavy breathing and headache are the first signs of CO_2 build up.

Despite the bad name given to oxygen rebreathing apparatus, usually by those who have never used it or by those that have used it without proper training and a knowledge of its limitations, the author has trained hundreds of divers in its use, over many years, without any incident whatever. It is true that the recognised limitations for oxygen rebreathing apparatus have always been most carefully observed, and a limit of 25-ft depth is never exceeded. But then most things that are worth doing require an observance of limitations of one sort or another.

There are great individual differences in susceptibility to

oxygen poisoning, and an individual's tolerance can vary from day to day. Oxygen poisoning is a result of the increase in the partial pressure of oxygen in the blood, which affects the respiratory centre of the brain. Temperature is also a factor, but it is depth (pressure), exercise, and an excess of CO_2 that influence a diver's susceptibility to oxygen poisoning. The average person does not suffer any ill effects when using an oxygen rebreather for periods of one hour, providing exercise is kept to a minimum. If light work is involved the duration of the descent should be limited to half an hour.

In an emergency only, short periods at depths in excess of 33 ft (2 atmospheres) may be exceeded with a reasonable expectation of avoiding oxygen poisoning.

Depth not exceeding	Duration not to exceed	Require ascent to 10 ft for periods not less than
50 ft	15 minutes	1 minute
60 ft	10 minutes	2 minutes
70 ft	7 minutes	5 minutes

Even so, oxygen poisoning may be experienced between 25 ft and 33 ft under conditions of exertion, as a small partial pressure of CO_2 (2 per cent of 1 atmosphere) can aggravate the onset of oxygen poisoning.

As a safeguard against the possibility of any nitrogen being present in the system due to careless venting of the breathing bag and lungs or to poor quality oxygen, it is wise to expel all gas from the breathing bag and flush up with fresh oxygen from the cylinder at least once every fifteen minutes. This can be done underwater quite conveniently.

As the diver is breathing pure oxygen, and as the level of CO_2 present is low, the diver can, if necessary, survive for quite a long period without breathing. In the event of exhausting the cylinder and breathing bag of oxygen, it is still possible to surface quite slowly, remembering, however, to allow the expanding oxygen in the lungs to vent harmlessly away through mouth or nose.

No hydrocarbon oil or grease must be used on any oxygen apparatus as they combine with the oxygen spontaneously, resulting in an explosion.

Silicone oil or grease, or glycerine, may be used sparingly for any necessary lubrication.

6

STANDARD DIVING APPARATUS

As its name implies, it is the standard diving apparatus for commercial underwater work. Its design has changed little during the last fifty years and differs from previously described apparatus in that the diver's head and shoulders are encased in a rigid structure, which acts as a diving bell, hence the American term 'Hard Hat'. Air under pressure is pumped from the surface so that, even without a protective dress, the diver's head would be surrounded by air at water pressure. The helmet is connected with a watertight joint to a rigid shoulder structure known as the corselet. The helmet is screwed down to the corselet by means of an interrupted thread, so that a rotation of 45 degrees secures the helmet firmly to the corselet.

Air is fed into the helmet through a one-way valve, and then through a system of ducts, which ensures that the helmet is completely ventilated. The internal pressure in the helmet exceeds water pressure by approximately 1 psi, the actual pressure being manually varied by the diver adjusting the spring loaded exhaust valve on the right hand side of the helmet. Although in appearance the whole assembly indicates great strength, it is merely a matter of large safety factors, as the differential pressures inside and out are negligible. As there is always a small positive pressure inside the helmet, a small hole would only allow air to bubble out, rather than water in.

The corselet is bolted or fastened by various means to a heavy flexible dress made of several layers of rubberised material. The joint is waterproof, and the outlet valve is adjusted so that the internal pressure inflates the upper part of the dress in normal use. Due to this rather large volume of air, the standard diver requires a lot of lead ballast. On his feet he wears weighted boots

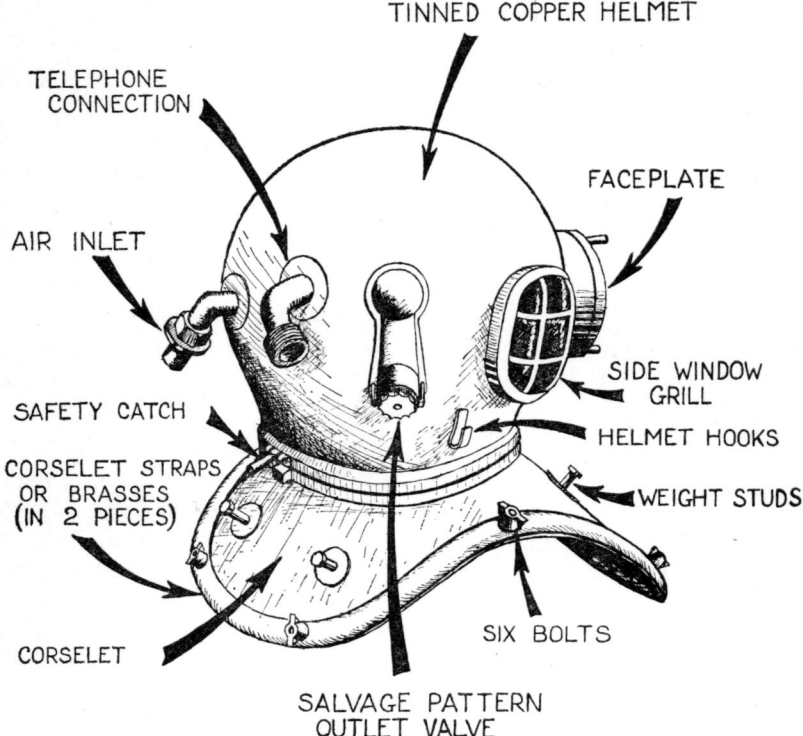

SIX-BOLT STANDARD DIVING HELMET

of 17 lb each, and on the front of his chest and on his back he carries another 80 lb.

Although out of the water the diver is virtually immobile, once submerged he is most comfortable. There is plenty of room in the dress for warm underclothes, and the helmet is most luxurious. The diver is not handicapped by having to use a mouthpiece, and he breathes as naturally and easily as on the surface. A two-way microphone-receiver telephone unit is fitted in the helmet, which is a great boon in serious underwater work. This comfort and the robustness of the apparatus is inclined to give the diver a false sense of security, for any safety involved is only

Standard Diving Apparatus

the outcome of good training and its assimilation by divers and attendants.

Before use, the equipment should be laid out and examined. The air hose must be connected up to either the hand pump, or the diver's panel, which in turn is connected to the source of supply, or the low pressure air reservoir when using a power driven compressor or compressed air cylinders. Every air pipe connection must have a leather washer fitted, including joints where two lengths of pipe are joined together. The joints must be tightened securely, using two spanners. The normal air pipe or hose used is sinking hose, but a length of floating hose is connected next to the diver. This prevents the hose from dragging across a rough bottom and 'snarling' from time to time. Sinking hose is black and floating hose is red.

Before attaching the air pipe to the left hand elbow on the helmet, blow air through to clear the pipe. Then place a finger over the end of the pipe and check that the pressure available will considerably exceed the depth of water involved. The diver's combined surface gauge indicates the depth at which the diver is working in feet, and the pressure in which he is working in pounds per square inch.

Turn off the air supply, and with the finger sealing off the pipe end, check that gauge pressure is maintained. This indicates that no leak exists. Before connecting to helmet elbow, insert finger and check that the spring loaded valve is free, and that it reseats instantly. This valve is vital to the diver's safety, for should the air pipe part with the valve stuck open, the air in the helmet and pipe would pour out, and without the support of air at water pressure internally, the full weight of the water above the diver would become effective, and he would suffer a violent 'squeeze', most likely fatal. At a depth of 66 ft he would be crushed by a total weight of 14 tons. The helmet being rigid, his body will tend to be crushed into it, and death would be instantaneous. Providing the valve is free to close, he would have a good chance of being hauled to the surface before being asphyxiated.

Having checked the valve, attach air hose to elbow on helmet and tighten securely with two spanners, taking care not to strain the elbow on the helmet. Next, connect the telephone breast rope to helmet and tighten with the special large spanner provided. The union nut must be tightened up firmly, or salt water will short the connections. If the helmet is near the telephone cabinet, with the front glass off and the power switched on, 'feed back' will cause a howl over the telephone. It indicates that the telephone is working.

It is assumed that the diving boat is already moored in position, with a shot rope conveniently close to the diving ladder, and the air hose and breast rope coiled down so that they can be paid out easily.

DRESSING THE DIVER

The diver, already dressed in heavy woollen underclothing, enters the diving dress feet first through the neck aperture, the attendant easing the dress over his shoulders, after soaping the diver's wrists and rubber cuffs. The diver can then slide his arms down the sleeves, and by putting each arm in turn between his knees, and keeping his fingers straight, can shoot his hands through the rubber cuffs.

The diver then sits down on a box or bench. The attendant slips the circular shoulder pad over the diver's head and works it over the shoulders inside the dress. This pad protects the shoulders from the metal corselet. The light inner collar or bib, is then held up round his face by the diver, whilst the attendant gently lowers the corselet over everything until it rests on his shoulders. The heavy rubber collar of the dress is them pulled out, and up, over the corselet, so that it overlaps all round. The attendant lifts the rubber collar at front and drops the holes in the rubber collar over the corselet studs, repeating at the back and finally at the sides.

The light inner collar is pulled up all round to prevent a fold being trapped between corselet and collar, and the hollow ended handle of the corselet spanner is pushed down over the corselet studs in order to make the rubber settle neatly round the protruding studs. The inner collar is then doubled over outwards around the diver's neck, leaving two or three inches protruding above the corselet.

The corselet straps or brasses are placed over the studs and the nuts run down loosely. With the six-bolt Admiralty Pattern

Standard Diving Apparatus

helmet and corselet, the rubber beadings should be eased into the recesses on the underside of the straps, before the middle wing nuts are tightened. With six- and twelve-bolt types, the middle nuts are tightened down first with the corselet spanner, and the nut over the joint is left until last. Do not overtighten, as the curve of the straps may be distorted.

Never leave corselet straps where they can be trodden on, or where the weights or boots may be dropped on them. When not in use, replace on corselet and run nuts down loosely.

The boots are now put on and fastened securely, with the buckles to the outside. Cuff rings can now be fitted over the joint between cuff and wrist. Cuff rings are more commonly called 'greys' or 'reds' depending on the type used.

The helmet, without front glass, is then very carefully placed over the diver's head, turned 45 degrees to the left, and settled down on to the seating washer. Straighten up helmet, and holding securely, but not by the air and telephone elbows, and after warning diver, screw up firmly to the right, until the hinged locking lever at the rear engages in its recess.

The air hose, leading from the left hand side of the helmet, is passed under the diver's left arm and the standing part secured to the grille of the left hand glass, with a lanyard so that no strain can be taken by the helmet fitting. The telephone breastrope is treated similarly. The knife belt is now fitted round the waist and passed through the loops of air hose and breast rope. This prevents any strain being taken by the air inlet and telephone elbows, should the lanyards come undone or break.

The air supply is now turned on, or the hand pumps started. The telephone is switched on and tested. The face glass is demisted, and when the diver is satisfied with the air supply he gives the word, and the face glass is screwed home firmly. The diver then stands up, moves to the ladder, and descends down it a step or two, the attendant holding him securely with the breast rope and air hose.

With the diver on the ladder, the attendant then fits the front weight by slipping the clip rings over the weight studs on the front of the corselet, and then the back weight whose lanyards are first led over the helmet hooks before clipping on to the same front weight studs. The lanyard from the back weight is passed inside the belt, between the diver's legs and hitched on to the front weight ring. It not only secures the weights, but acts as a jock strap. If ring clips are not being used, the back weight lanyards are brought over the helmet hooks, and passed through the front weight rings, and secured with a quick release bow hitch.

FIRST LESSON

All being secure, the diver receives a double tap on the helmet from the attendant, which indicates that he may submerge.

The attendant takes up the slack as the diver descends, to prevent any possibility of a serious squeeze, should the diver lose control and fall off the ladder or shot rope. A squeeze, through falling or descending faster than the pumps can cope with the increasing pressure, will crush the diver.

The diver just submerges and then closes his outlet valve, so that the attendant can watch for any leaks, which will be indicated by bubbles of air escaping. When the attendant is satisfied that all is well, he informs the diver by telephone or pre-arranged signal, and then draws him over to the shot rope. The air supply is increased above normal for descent, and the diver adjusts his valve so that he can slide down the shot rope effortlessly and under complete control. The air supply is increased as, due to descent into a greater pressure, the air in the dress and helmet is reduced in volume. The diver may have to stop on the shot rope and wait for the air supply to catch up with him.

The speed of descent of an experienced diver is only limited by his ability to clear his ears, and by the air supply being sufficient to prevent him being squeezed. In standard diving the ears can be cleared by pressing the nose against the inner collar, yawning or swallowing. A nose clip can be used if desired and knocked off on the collar when reaching the bottom to avoid distorting the diver's voice over the telephone.

On reaching the bottom, the diver informs the surface, and the air supply is reduced to his needs. Plain simple English is used over the telephone, as for radio telephone. Bad language merely informs all within hearing that he is badly trained, or suffering

Standard Diving Apparatus

from nervousness. A pair of earphones plugged into the telephone cuts out the public address type of speaker, so that the diver's communication can be confidential.

On his first descent, the diver under training having reached the bottom should adjust his outlet valve so that the corselet just lifts off his shoulders. Holding the shot rope, he has a look round as he becomes used to the apparatus. After a short period, he can experiment with his outlet valve, making himself heavy and light alternately. As confidence grows, he can take the distance line, which is coiled up and made fast to the shot rope a foot or two above the shot weight, and walk about on the bottom, uncoiling the distance line as he goes. For the first lesson, a clean hard bottom is desirable, in not more than 12 ft of water.

If the diver begins to pant, he requires more air. Using a telephone, the attendant will probably notice the panting before the diver becomes aware of it.

Having walked well away from the shot rope, the distance line will lead him back to it again, and it should be coiled neatly as the slack comes in.

At this stage the diver can practice a few essential hand signals on the breast rope, and should already have committed the following to memory.

1 pull	Stop or Attention
2 pulls	Lower away
3 pulls	Heave up
4 pulls	Come up, or Diver coming up
5 pulls	More air
6 pulls	Less air
7 pulls	Send assistance
8 pulls	Pull diver up
1 shake (consisting of twelve or more quick jerks or pulls) indicates that everything is all right	

When ascending or descending, one pull means stop, but on other occasions it means 'Attention—a signal will follow'. The recipient repeats one pull and waits for the signal. Having received the signal, he repeats it back before acting on it.

It is possible for the linesman or diver to receive an accidental 'One', which he repeats back. At the other end the receiver thinks he is being called and he repeats 'One' back. This can go on until one of the two suddenly realises what has happened and he then gives the long shake to indicate that all is well as far as he is concerned. Unfortunately there is no standard code of hand signals, and the ones shown here are only intended for emergency use, in the event of a telephone failure. They are the old Siebe, Gorman signals, as used at the British Underwater Centre. Naval dockyard divers use a much more comprehensive code. However, any signals in use must be well learnt by both diver and linesman.

The linesman pays out, and takes in the slack of the breast rope and air hose as required, allowing the diver sufficient to work, but never allowing surplus coils to lie around on the bottom. Apart from the ever present danger of fouling, any slackness would mean that a diver, walking into a hole, or slipping off the deck of a ship down into a hold, or over the side, would suffer a nasty squeeze.

The diver having returned to the shot rope, informs the surface that he is coming up. The diver adjusts his outlet valve so that he can ascend the shot rope with little effort, the attendant taking in the slack and, in an emergency, helping the diver a little. To get the right adjustment is not easy at first, and to prevent any possibility of 'blowing up' under the diving boat, he should wrap his legs around the shot rope and keep a firm hold with his hands. The Salvage type outlet valve has a spindle projecting from the centre of the adjusting screw-cap, so that finger pressure on this spindle will close the valve immediately. He can use it when ascending the shot rope, and when in danger of 'blowing up' he only has to release the pressure. It is also useful in that he can quieten the bubbles momentarily when listening to the telephone.

The attendant's responsibility for the diver's safety is paramount and he must not allow his attention to wander. He must anticipate trouble both above and below water, and must keep an eye on the diver's gauge and air supply. A sudden increase in depth shown on the gauge indicates that the diver has fallen into a greater pressure of water. If he does not reply to signals, haul him up, but not too quickly. A decrease shown on the gauge means that he is coming up, 'blowing up' out of control, or the

Standard Diving Apparatus

apparatus has failed. If he is coming up, gather in the slack breast rope and air hose, but if he says he is all right and the pressure continues to fall, call him up immediately.

Once again on the ladder, the front and back leads are removed, but the face glass must not be removed, or the air supply stopped or turned off until he is safely aboard.

Undressing the diver more or less follows the reverse procedure for dressing. To remove the hands from the cuffs, the diver's hands and wrists are soaped again, and the attendant holds down the bottom of the sleeves, one at a time, with two hands in the region of the diver's knees. The diver pulls up his arm until the rubber cuff is turned inside out in the sleeve, and then with a sharp jerk his hand will slip up through the cuff quite easily.

It is advisable to wash down the dress and metal parts with fresh water, to remove all traces of salt. The dress is then hung up in the shade to dry, and the helmet and corselet wiped dry and placed in the sun or in a warm dry corner.

SECOND LESSON

On the driver's second descent he can practise sliding down the shot rope a little faster, as time saved descending to an appreciable depth can be spent doing useful work on the bottom, with only the same stage decompression, as the duration of the dive is timed when the diver leaves the surface.

Again on the bottom, with the valve adjusted nicely, usually about half to three-quarters of a turn, the diver can practise falling forward on to his hands. The fall is in slow motion and is a very pleasant sensation. Whilst lying down, first lie on the left hand side. With the head held up slightly, there is no risk of the dress filling up with air, and the diver 'blowing up' helplessly to the surface. Then try lying on the right hand side, when the outlet valve will be down. The dress will soon begin to inflate, and the diver will notice that the air begins to lift the dress along his back. By opening the outlet valve fully, and lifting head occasionally to clear dress of surplus air, it is possible to continue working without 'blowing up'. If too much air accumulates it will be necessary to kneel up quickly if control is not to be lost.

In not more than 12 ft of water it is possible to practise valve control by closing valve and floating to surface, having made sure that the diving boat is not overhead. As the diver begins to rise, quick, delicate work with the valve will be necessary to

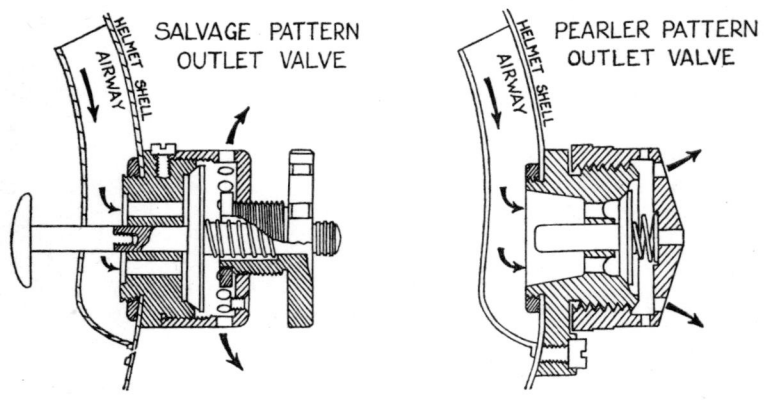

Outlet valves: (*left*) salvage pattern; (*right*) pearler pattern

prevent the expanding air in the dress from taking charge. The aim should be to rise vertically and float on the surface with the front glass half submerged. At first it is easy for the diver to over inflate, and he is soon helpless in a 'blown up' condition, floating horizontally on the surface. The drill for a diver having 'blown up' is then put into practice.

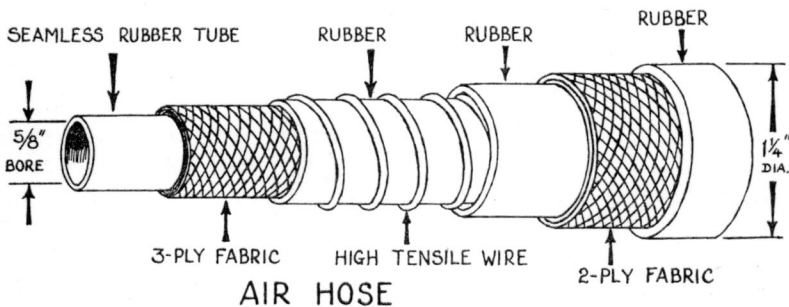

Standard Diving Apparatus

The attendant stops the pumps or the air supply for the moment and draws the floating diver towards the diving boat. Even if he can, which is doubtful, the diver must not attempt to open his outlet valve, for if he was some way from the boat, and in deep water, the resulting fall and squeeze would probably cure him of diving for good. Actually a fall in 12 ft of water would do no harm, but the resulting 'nip' gives some idea of the weight of water. It can be practised during training, but the diver must not develop the habit of opening the valve on 'blowing up' out of control.

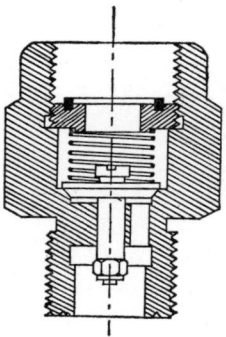

INLET VALVE

The attendant having drawn the diver to the ladder, makes the breast rope and air hose secure, and then reaches over and fully opens the outlet valve. To hasten deflation he can also open the 'spit' cock, which is on the left front of the helmet, and taking an arm he can open the cuff a little, which is even more effective. As the dress deflates, the diver's feet and legs begin to sink, and he can soon help himself on to the ladder. The pumps are then started, or the air supply turned on, and the diver can be sent down again. If, of course, he had blown up accidentally from any appreciable depth then he must be sent down immediately and decompressed as required by the tables. If the diver is feeling the first symptoms of the bends, they will pass off when he is once more under pressure. Even if unconscious or injured, perhaps from 'blowing up' under the boat, he must be sent down again after any necessary first aid.

Still under training, the diver descends again to the bottom. He should now adjust his valve so that he is very nearly in a state of neutral buoyancy. In this condition he will be able to jump effortlessly over obstructions and ropes. An accidental 'blow up' on this exercise will familiarise him with the preliminary sensation of losing control. Keep well away from the diving boat and ladder when any risk of 'blowing up' exists. Further descents for the purpose of practising simulated searches, mechanical assembly, and the underwater sawing of wood and metal will complete the basic practical training with standard diving apparatus.

If a diver loses his distance line, he can, by taking hold of the breast rope and hose, and facing the run of them, be drawn or led back to a position under the diving boat. He may then find the shot rope, but if not, he can be hauled to the surface by the attendant, keeping his valve well open to avoid any chance of 'blowing up' under the boat. An attendant can direct the diver by asking him to face the run of his breast rope and hose, and then directing him to move at 90 degrees to the right, or 45 degrees to the left and so on, conning him by his surface bubbles, always allowing for the set of any current during the time the bubbles are rising to the surface.

The diver must always be conscious of the position of the shot rope or other obstruction, and avoid getting foul of them. If he does become foul, he must think back and reverse his movements, keeping cool and taking things easy. Panic and exertion will always complicate matters. If it is only the shot rope that is entangled the attendant can haul the whole lot to the surface, diver, hoses, shot rope and all. If hopelessly foul on the bottom, a second diver may have to descend to render assistance, preferably in self-contained apparatus. It may even be necessary to detach a fouled air pipe, and refit another one, the spring loaded valve holding back the air in the helmet during the change over. The spare hose would have to be attached with air flowing continuously.

Page 71 (*left*) Constant volume suit; (*right*) Dreadnought oil proof standard dress and twelve-bolt corselet

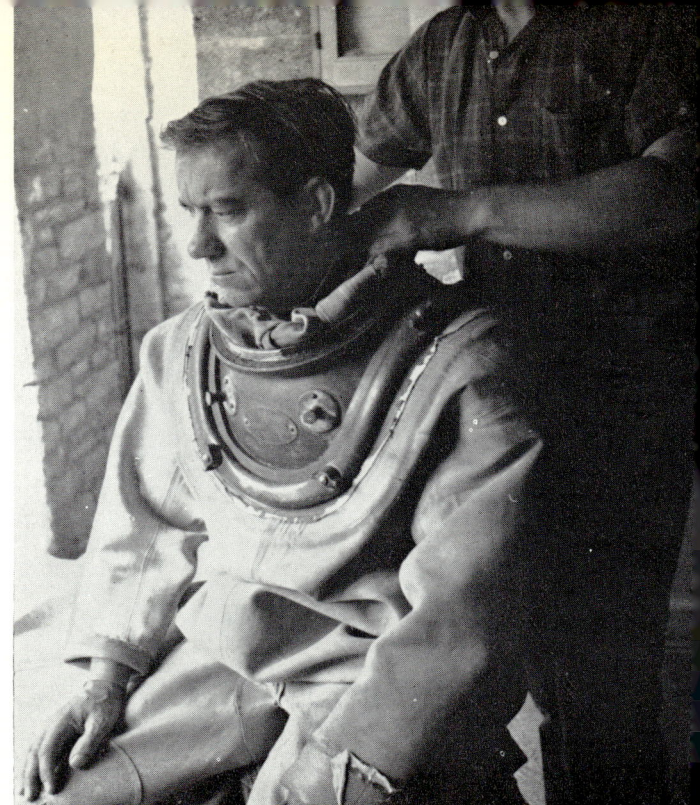

Page 72 (*above*) Tucking the inner collar or 'bib' into the six-bolt Admiralty pattern corselet; (*below*) deep sea leads for standard diver, 40 lb each

7

AIR SUPPLY

HAND PUMPS

THE standard divers' hand pump, of traditional design, is still in common use. They are simple in design, bordering on the primitive, but they work effectively down to 100 ft, and above all else, are extremely reliable. Their great drawback in Britain or America is their extravagance in 'manpower', and at today's hourly rate it is cheaper to use power or compressed air cylinders.

A standard pattern used by the British Navy and many contractors, is the two-cylinder double-acting pump for two divers in shallow water, or one diver in deep water. A four-cylinder single-acting pump is supplied for similar duties. For one diver a three-cylinder single-acting pump is popular for harbour work and for pearl and sponge diving. For one diver in moderate depths, both single-cylinder double-acting, and two-cylinder single-acting pumps are available.

They are complete in strong cases, which match their rugged construction. Built of gunmetal and hard wood, they will, with reasonable maintenance, last a life-time. The author has seen hand pumps originally built in 1904, looking and working like new after a factory overhaul. A gauge is built into the hard-wood casing, and indicates the diver's depth in feet, and the pressure of the surrounding water in pounds per square inch.

Pumps having a capacity sufficient for two divers, include a distributing cock which will supply the two divers with an air supply whilst working at different depths, each diver having independent gauges; or one diver at a considerable depth and taking the entire output from all cylinders. A single diver, when using a pump for two divers, must have his air pipe connected to the left hand outlet. When the distributing cock lever is moved over to 'one diver—deep water', the right hand outlet supply is cut off.

A water jacket surrounds each cylinder which can be filled and refilled from time to time, with cold water when used in hot weather or with hot water when used in cold weather. Depths below 40 ft are considered deep diving.

The diver's combined gauge, like all other gauges, is liable to have an error. As it is important to know the correct depth of a diver, any error must be known, and each gauge requires calibrating. From the end of the air pipe, measure off 10 ft lengths and mark them off to 60 ft. Make fast a sufficiently heavy sinker with a rolling hitch to the end of the air pipe and lower to each mark in turn. There must be no current running if the diving boat is moored, and there must be little or no wind blowing whether moored or drifting. Supply air at each mark until bubbles rise to the surface, and then note gauge reading. Tabulate the true depths against gauge depths and paste the calibration table alongside each gauge.

Multi-cylinder hand pumps have been supplied with an alternate power drive, either petrol engine or electrical, by Siebe Gorman & Co Ltd. As four men are required on the pumps, even for depths of only 50 or 60 ft, the economy of power is obvious.

A convenient and economic method of supplying a standard diver or a surface supply demand valve diver, is to use three 160-cu-ft compressed air cylinders. Two of them contain air at high pressure, fed by way of a two-way manifold, through a reducing valve, to the third cylinder, which is maintained at approximately 120 psi. This low pressure air is fed to the diver's panel when used with standard gear, or direct to the diver in the case of demand valve apparatus. Having a two-way manifold with cocks, the high pressure cylinders can be replaced when empty, without interrupting the supply to the diver.

POWER COMPRESSORS

Several types of power driven compressors are available for use with standard gear or other surface supply apparatus. When

Air Supply

power is depended upon entirely, an air reservoir of sufficient capacity to get the diver or divers up in the event of power failure is absolutely essential.

If the diver happened to be foul, the usual low pressure type of reservoir might not be sufficient so, if available, a 2,000 psi cylinder feeding through a reducing valve, is much more practical. It also takes up less room in a small boat, whilst allowing for lengthy decompression.

If the standard diver is not foul and is close to his shot rope, the danger of an air supply failure is not serious as he can make a slow controlled ascent on the expanding air in his dress, with only a little initial help from the attendant to reach a condition of neutral buoyancy. Once this point is reached it is necessary to valve off the expanding air in order to avoid blowing up.

In choosing a compressor, it must be remembered that the pressure of water increases approximately $\frac{1}{2}$ lb per square inch for every foot of depth, and before the air can even reach the diver this pressure has to be exceeded. In fact the pressure available should be approximately twice the pressure at the working depth. Not only the pressure must be adequate, but the capacity in cubic feet per minute must also be ample at the required pressure. A standard diver requires air for ventilating his helmet, apart from that required to ventilate his lungs and satisfy his oxygen want. He requires 1·5 cu ft at the surface, and an extra 1·5 cu ft for every 33 ft of depth.

It may be necessary to send down a second diver to help a diver in trouble, so it is wise to have a compressor with a capacity that will cope with any such emergency.

The quantity of air required by a diver using surface supply demand valve apparatus will be the same as that required by a free diver using self-contained apparatus.

HIGH PRESSURE COMPRESSORS

For self-contained apparatus requiring compressed atmospheric air at 2,000 psi the compressor problem is not easily overcome. Any compressor of this type is a very expensive and complicated piece of machinery. It will require three separate stages and each stage is equivalent to a low pressure compressor in itself, having a compression ratio of 5:1. As the compression of air generates heat, and as hot air occupies a greater space than cold, interstage cooling is necessary if the compressor is to be efficient. Also, as it would be difficult to restart with the high pressure air trapped in the system, automatic unloaders are a necessity.

For self-contained apparatus, the air must be dry to prevent icing up in the reducing valve. This means a silica-gel drier must be included, and if the compressor is to be oil lubricated, it will also require an efficient filter unit. As the continual breathing of oil-laden air will seriously affect the health of the diver, all compressed air supplied by oil lubricated compressors must be efficiently filtered through a medium such as activated charcoal or alumina. Water lubricated compressors are even more complicated and expensive. Water lubrication is essential for compressing pure oxygen, but oil lubrication is quite satisfactory for the filling of compressed air cylinders.

However, it is important that an oil lubricated compressor is not driven beyond its rated rpm. In fact for the charging of breathing apparatus, it is much better to run it well below the maker's recommended rpm. If an oil lubricated compressor is allowed to run too hot, there is a danger of the lubricating oil 'dieseling', and as one of the products of combustion is carbon monoxide (CO), this very poisonous gas would be present in the diver's cylinders. A suitable high flash-point lubricating oil will reduce the danger.

It is an interesting point that the pressure of 2,000 psi is ten times higher than the pressure to which the air in a diesel engine is compressed, but it means little really, as the compression ratio of each separate stage is quite low, and there is little danger if the compressor is run well within its rated capacity.

Aqualung-type cylinders can be refilled at commercial gas company depots throughout the world, or at the British Underwater Centre at Dartmouth. Siebe, Gorman & Co Ltd supply a hand booster pump, which will boost compressed air from commercial cylinders to the 2,000 psi required. This pump is distilled water lubricated, and can be used for filling the oxygen cylinders used with oxygen rebreathing apparatus. Even when the oxygen pressure in the storage cylinder is low, only a few strokes are required to top up the 4-cu-ft cylinders.

Air Supply

Pure oxygen must not be pumped with anything but water-lubricated pumps, as oil or grease in contact with oxygen under high pressure will result in a violent explosion.

For shallow water work, a converted gas mask, fed by a light rubber hose from the surface is excellent. Only a low pressure compressor is required, but it must have a capacity of 3 or more cu ft per minute.

A more convenient arrangement is the demand valve surface supply apparatus. This consists of a simple demand valve, which is mounted on a harness high on the diver's back, the diver having inhale and exhale corrugated tubes and mouthpiece, as with an aqualung. A pressure of about 120 psi is still required, but the capacity required will only be $1\frac{1}{2}$ to 2 cu ft per minute. It is wise to invest in a compressor that will supply more air than is normally required.

When using an internal-combustion engine as a power unit for driving a compressor, the exhaust fumes must be led well clear of the air intake. In a steady wind, with the engine exhaust to loo'ard, there is no problem, but in a calm or light variable wind, the contaminated exhaust fumes can hang around persistently. As CO is present in exhaust fumes, and as the poisonous effect of any gas increases under pressure, the nuisance must be given serious consideration.

Demand valve surface supply apparatus, being so economical in air, can take its supply from a reducing valve screwed straight into a compressed air cylinder. The reducing valve is normally set to supply air at 120 psi. The 160-cu-ft cylinder will have four times the endurance of the standard aqualung cylinder.

Having no high pressure compressor, or booster pump, the individual or club can fill self-contained cylinders by decanting from three or more cylinders. As the cylinders when full are at 2,000 psi it is impossible to put 2,000 psi into the breathing apparatus cylinders by merely decanting. However, given sufficient cylinders, the difference will be negligible. Presuming only three cylinders are available at one time, balance off the aqualung cylinder from No 1 cylinder, then top up a little more from No 2 and finish by topping up from No 3. The pressure in No 2 cylinder will only be a little down and No 3 will still be nearly full. The aqualung cylinder will be at the same pressure as No 3 cylinder, and for all practical purposes can be considered full.

Having emptied the aqualung cylinder, it is balanced off on No 1 cylinder again. No 1 cylinder is then replaced by a new full one. The aqualung cylinder is then topped up from No 2 and No 3 and finally from the new cylinder. On the next occasion No 2 cylinder will be balanced off first and replaced by another new one and so on. A specially made manifold will facilitate decanting, as the topping up process will only require the opening and shutting of valves instead of attaching and detaching the aqualung cylinder to each individual cylinder.

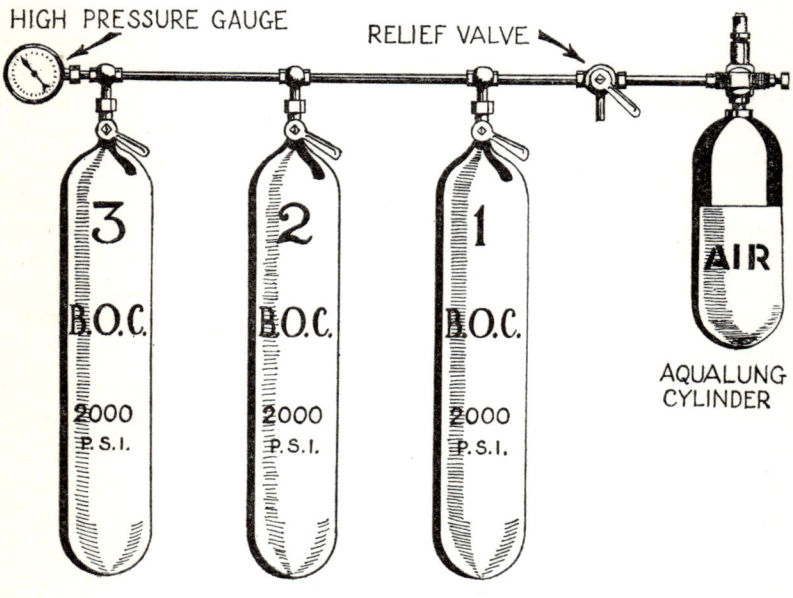

Filling the cylinder

8

DEEP DIVING AND COAST DIVING

In the past, depths exceeding 40 ft were considered deep diving, and deep sea divers were a race apart from their less qualified shallow water brethren of docks, harbours and inland waterways. In fact many shallow water divers received no training or theoretical knowledge at all, and graduated to diving after a practical apprenticeship in tending their predecessors. There is little doubt that these stalwarts have been of more commercial value to mankind, plodding on with their less romantic work, than the more spectacular deep sea salvage diver. Today, with the advent of self-contained demand valve apparatus, 40 ft is considered nothing at all. After suitable training, elderly men and women, and children of either sex, play around happily at this level.

In theory this self-contained apparatus is as safe as any underwater apparatus in use, and undoubtedly, in knowledgeable and experienced hands, remarkably deep descents can be made. Unfortunately, 'we do not know what we do not know', and several intrepid but inexperienced free divers have plunged into the depths, with little thought of nitrogen narcosis and none at all of oxygen poisoning through breathing atmospheric air below 300 ft. After considerable experience, free-divers can safely work and play around the 150-ft level.

The quantity of compressed air and the number of cylinders carried on the diver's back, need not get out of hand, as it is tending to in America. The bulk of the air required for a deep descent is not used on the bottom, but is required for stage decompression on the ascent. The author has used a Siebe, Gorman CABA with two 40-cu-ft cylinders, and a low pressure pipe leading from the low pressure air supply between the reducing valve and the demand valve to a position on his chest.

After a deep descent, with the air supply running low, the diver can move up to 60 ft, at 25 ft per minute, where he finds the end of a hose leading from a reducing valve up in the boat above. The reducing valve is fitted to a two-way manifold coupled to a BOC compressed air cylinder and an oxygen cylinder. The diver signals on the hose and the attendant turns on the air supply at 120 psi. When a continuous stream of air is bubbling from the hose, the diver plugs the hose on to the pipe on his chest. Air is then fed from the surface straight to the diver's demand valve. The diver's cylinders are then turned off, the air remaining being saved for an emergency.

The whole decompression period is completed on the surface supply, and the stage decompression controlled by the surface crew by hauling the air hose and diver up together. The decompression periods can be shortened by feeding the diver with oxygen from 30 ft upwards. Stage decompression 'stops' required on atmospheric air can be divided by 2·5 when using oxygen.

With self-contained apparatus having no convenient surface supply tapping, the same system can be used. A standard aqualung mouthpiece fitted on one end of the 'T' piece with a corrugated rubber breathing tube, and a rubber spear valve on the other. The tube is fitted to the end of the surface hose pipe. When air is flowing from the mouthpiece, the diver removes his apparatus mouthpiece and inserts the hose mouthpiece, and continues on the surface supply. If he prevents the corrugated tubes of his apparatus from floating up above him, he will not waste the air in the cylinders, but can save it for an emergency as before. A lot of air will be wasted from the spear valve on the hose, but they have air to spare above.

There is nothing new in breathing straight from a hose pipe. In the world of showmanship, girls used to stage tea parties, etc in quite deep water, using no apparatus at all. Trained to hold their breath for long periods, they only required an occasional breath from a dangling hose pipe at quite lengthy intervals, and they had no such luxury as a mouthpiece and a spear valve to exhale through.

For really deep diving special mixtures of oxygen and helium are necessary. A diver breathing helium does not suffer from the mental aberration caused by nitrogen-narcosis, and with a reduced supply of oxygen can descend further before the danger of oxygen poisoning becomes the limiting factor. As helium has high heat conductive properties, when the diver's body is partly surrounded by it as in standard gear, he loses a great amount of body heat and the dress has to be electrically heated. The use of helium in self-contained apparatus, being only breathed and not surrounding the free-diver's body, would not have the disadvantage to the same extent.

It has been suggested that the effect of nitrogen-narcosis might be retarded by a pre-dive period spent breathing pure oxygen at atmospheric pressure. It would not be practical to achieve a total elimination of nitrogen within the body before descent, but two or three hours on pure oxygen before descent would reduce the nitrogen present in the body, most likely retarding the onset of nitrogen narcosis.

Beyond 300 ft the effects of oxygen poisoning can be eliminated, when using multi-cylinder self-contained apparatus, by having one cylinder filled with a special mixture containing a lower partial pressure of oxygen. Descent to the danger level would then be made on a normal mixture, the diver changing over to the special mixture for the duration of the descent beyond 200 ft, changing back again on ascent.

Beyond 150 ft even an experienced free-driver should make use of a safety line and a shot rope. The surface attendant can then give one pull every minute or less, to be answered by the diver, failing which the diver is hauled to the surface. The safety line can be marked off at 10 ft intervals from the diver, for decompression purposes. A full face mask must be worn, so that in the event of the diver convulsing or becoming unconscious, he would not drown.

Descents to these depths must not be treated lightly, as a lot of careful planning and calculation are essential if the adventure is to be anything more than a death or glory newspaper stunt. A shot rope is necessary for deep descents, as the energy required in swimming down 100 ft or so can be most exhausting. A lump of expendable iron will help. If long decompression stops are required, the shot rope is also needed to guide the diver back to the supplementary air and/or oxygen supply.

Using self-contained diving apparatus, it is better to work with

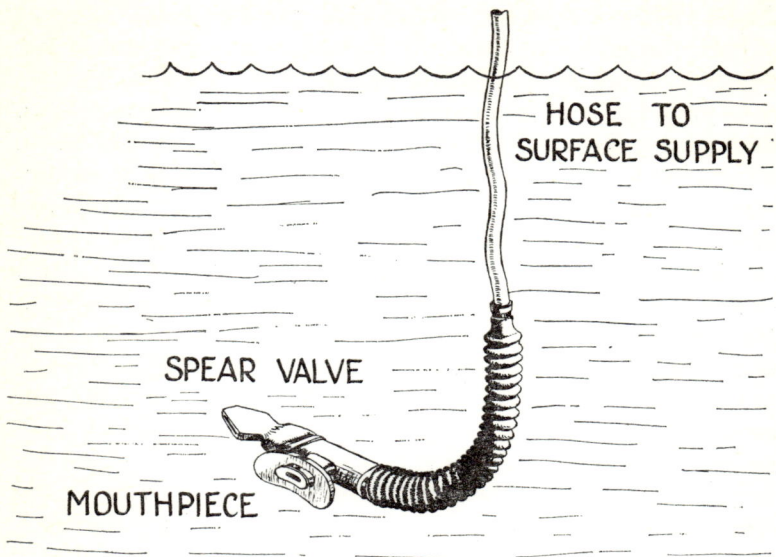

DECOMPRESSION - SURFACE SUPPLY

a slack shot rope in a heaving sea, as the effect of a vertical shot rope, which is alternatively rigid and then slack, is most disconcerting. When using standard gear, the author prefers to have the sinker of the shot rope several feet off the bottom, to suit the surface conditions, as the heave of the diving boat is less troublesome than the slackening and tensioning of the shot rope.

For deep sea diving a substantial vessel is required. It is a well known saying among seamen that 'the larger the ship, the easier the ride'. It must be remembered, however, that a boat must be anchored when diving on a particular site, and the larger the boat the heavier the anchors and chain will be, and they need man-handling—unless funds run to boats of such a size that they are equipped with a power windlass. We are considering, of course, the problem as it applies to sporting and small commercial diving units, and not naval or large deep sea salvage operations.

Deep Diving and Coast Diving 83

Boats of up to 10 tons, under quiet conditions, can usually hold their position in deep water by anchoring with a shot rope and a pig of lead or iron ballast. A line can be 'rolling hitched' to the shot rope below water level and led back to the diving ladder as a guide for the diver. Few small boats have sufficient chain to anchor in deep water. In order to hold its position in anything but tideless, calm conditions, a boat requires a scope of chain or warp of a length equal to five times the depth of water it is anchored in.

A beamy boat will be stiff in smooth water, and will have a minimum of heel when the diving ladder is abeam. Even so, a heavily ballasted diver, with two attendants leaning over the gunwale, will put one side down considerably. A boat of moderate beam can have the diving ladder mounted on the transom stern, when there will be no tendency to heel, and it will have an easier motion in a seaway.

The ladder is a most important item of a diver's equipment, and in a special diving boat, it should be designed and fitted very carefully. A broken ladder, with a standard diver still in the water, is more than a nuisance, and not a little ingenuity will be required in getting him aboard. Even with a diver using self-contained apparatus it may be necessary to remove the equipment whilst still in the water, and heave the diver and lung up separately.

Always remember that problems appear much smaller when viewed from dry land, where everything is rigid and morale is high. It is often the over-enthusiastic divers that are rigid after an hour or two at sea. An experienced seaman in command of the expedition is the best insurance against an adventure turning into a tragic accident.

In northern latitude waters light can be expected at 200-ft depth with the sun high in the sky, but in January at midday it is quite dark at 150 ft. Under certain conditions such as 'black' diving (total darkness), it may not be possible to keep a check on the contents gauge, but an increase in the breathing effort will warn the diver that his supply is running low. When a cylinder empties underwater, it is only empty in the sense that no more air can be drawn from it. An immediate ascent to a lesser pressure will produce a little more air, until the pressure in the cylinder is again nearly that of ambient pressure. For this reason there is no need to make a 'free ascent' when the air runs low, although it will be necessary to terminate that particular descent.

A single cylinder aqualung is considered safer for the inexperienced free-diver than a twin, as the 40 or 50-cu-ft cylinder regardless of the depth, will not be sufficient for the diver to require stage decompression. He will be forced to ascend due to his air supply running out. However, he will be required to ascend at the standard decompression speed of 25 ft per minute, which must be observed for descents greater than 33 ft.

A second descent within twelve hours is quite another thing, for the duration must be added to any other within that period, and then the decompression tables may well call for some 'stops'. Only one descent beyond 150 ft is permitted within any one twenty-four-hour period.

When using multi-cylinder aqualungs, or very large singles, it is possible to stay down long enough to require stage decompression, and yet not have the reserve of air left to carry out the stage decompression called for.

MIXTURE DIVING

It is the mixture of the gas breathed that limits the maximum depth to which it is safe to descend. Neglecting nitrogen narcosis, the limit for compressed air diving is that at which the partial pressure of oxygen in this mixture of gases comes up to 2 atmospheres pressure. With pure oxygen we have a limit of 33 ft, so with air we have a limit of approximately 300 ft, because air being 1/5 oxygen we can descend to 10 atmospheres pressure before the partial pressure of oxygen comes up to 2 atmospheres.

We can, therefore, choose a mixture to suit the working depth, that will be just within the safe limit as regards oxygen poisoning and yet contain a minimum percentage of nitrogen, which in turn reduces the absorption of this inert gas within the diver's body.

Mixture oxygen/air	Maximum Depth	Proportions in atmospheric pressure
60/40	82 ft	59 oxygen 61 air at 120 ats
40/60	140 ft	29 ,, 91 ,, ,, ,, ,,
32/68	180 ft	18 ,, 102 ,, ,, ,, ,,

Deep Diving and Coast Diving

Apart from being extremely hazardous, descents beyond 300 ft should be confined to well equipped teams of experienced divers. Beyond these depths the percentage of oxygen in the mixture is reduced to less than 10 per cent, which will take the diver below 600 ft, but this quantity of oxygen is not sufficient at surface pressure.

COAST DIVING

Swim-diving from a beach or rocks, using breathing apparatus, can be very pleasant or it can be hazardous, depending on the local conditions. If no boat or float is available, the diver must always bear in mind that a return has to be made, and due allowance given for dwindling energy, loss of body heat, and the compressed air supply. A breathing tube should always be included in the equipment, so that in the event of being caught in a tidal current too strong to 'make way' against, whilst hampered with diving apparatus, he can divert himself from his original plan, and by extending his endurance with the breathing tube, make tracks for an alternative landing down current.

Never swim-dive with heavy breathing apparatus through heavy surf. As the internal motion inside a breaking wave is sluggish at its base compared with the shoreward rush of its crest, it is always possible to swim seawards by diving deep into the base. On attempting to land through heavy surf, however, the diver finds himself being swept up the beach on the crest of a wave, to be dropped heavily on receding pebbles or sand. Struggling and stumbling under the weight of his gear, and falling over his swim-finned feet, the following wave drops on him with incredible force, and before he can gather his wits, he is being rolled up and down the beach in a most undignified manner, and in not a little danger.

When hunting or fishing off the shore, any sort of boat or raft is better than nothing at all, and even a canoe can tow a tired and frightened swim-diver to safety. A small buoyant surf-board, equipped with double-bladed paddles (secured) is very satisfactory for the lone hunter. An attachment that will hold the harpoon gun or spear can easily be fitted. On sighting his quarry, he slides off the board with his weapon, keeping contact with a light line made fast to his upper arm, or even letting it float freely under good conditions. The board moves effortlessly, and being so low in the water, holds very little wind. To board again, the diver approaches from one end and submerges it, sliding the board down as he pulls himself forward on his stomach. In this position, his legs and swim fins can be used as a propeller for short distances, or he can kneel or sit up and paddle.

Rubber inflatable dinghies can be useful, but they can also behave very badly, and in a strong wind they can take charge altogether. With the rubber floor cut out, and a foothold made by slinging a weighted plank below at a suitable depth, it could be an excellent safe diving platform. A Carley float would be even better, but that has not the great advantage of deflation for transport.

9

PROTECTIVE CLOTHING

WITH standard diving apparatus there is little choice of dress except that light-weight or heavy-weight 'salvus' materials are available. For cold water work a diving dress is supplied with the arms ending in mits. The hands are then dry and by raising an arm occasionally, with plenty of air in the dress, air can circulate round the fingers.

A cuff is also available for the normal type of diving dress, that will take a stiff metal ring designed to keep the wrist open. A special gauntlet diving glove is then drawn over the ring and clamped with a metal band.

In cold water, when working with bare hands, it helps to immerse the hands in a bucket of water before descent. When they begin to go numb, remove them, and then by swinging and rubbing, get the blood circulating again. In a few minutes they will be tingling with warmth, and will stay warm much longer underwater.

For protecting the hands from abrasions or filth, rubber gloves are supplied with wrist seals that seal over the normal cuff. But they help very little in protecting the hands from cold, as rubber itself is a poor insulator. Woollen gloves worn underneath do help a little. For use with self-contained underwater swimming apparatus, rubber gloves are available with webbing between the fingers.

When swimming underwater in a tight-fitting wet suit, or more or less naked, the use of arms and hands is not required, but with the drag of a full waterproof suit (together with the extra lead required to cancel out the extra buoyancy of underclothes, etc), the arm used with a breast-stroke movement can help considerably in propelling the swim-diver through the water. The webbed gloves can then be of real service.

Ordinary rubber kitchen gloves are perfect for protecting the hands from barnacles and rocks. Being thin and having all the fingers, they are hardly noticed in use, and are so cheap that they can be considered expendable.

Standard diving dresses have changed little over the years and it is difficult to see how they could be improved. New plastic materials may eventually replace the rubberised twill, but there is no certainty about that. For self-contained diving, the demand valve surface supply apparatus, the old wartime 'Sladen' suit, manufactured by Siebe, Gorman & Co Ltd is most luxurious. It was developed by the Admiralty for operational use and is rather expensive. It is a one-piece suit with a heavy rubber hood and a built-in face mask. It is entered from the front, legs first, followed by the arms and shoulders. The rubber helmet is then lifted from the back and placed over the head. The tubular trunk entry is then hanging from the chest. It is held up by the top edge, so that it hangs vertically. The rubber is folded back four or five inches, and then folded vertically, concertina fashion, each lap being approximately $2\frac{1}{2}$ in. A diver's plain cuff ring is then stretched over the folds, and it is then placed in the clamp and tightened evenly by hand. A final light tightening with the special key spanner supplied, completes the operation.

Up to date, the most practical dry suit for use with any self-contained apparatus, both for underwater swimming and shallow water diving, is the two-piece swim suit, originally designed for the wartime frogman. It consists of a bottom half in the form of trousers with feet, and a rubber latex skirt hanging from the waistband. These skirts must be seamless, or they will leak when rolled together. A top half, in the same material, includes a rubber latex dipped hood, with an open aperture for the face. It also has a rubber skirt, which hangs from the waist, overlapping the skirt on the trousers.

Long woollen underclothing, or a track suit, are worn underneath. The diver dresses in his woollens and socks, and then gets into the trousers. The top half of the suit is entered arms first, the fingers being held together and pointed, whilst an attendant stretches the light rubber cuffs wide open, with the first two fingers of each hand turned outwards. With arms in and wrists through the rubber cuffs, the suit is then pulled gently

Page 89 (*above*) Control panel for one standard diver; (*below*) Cressi oxygen rebreather

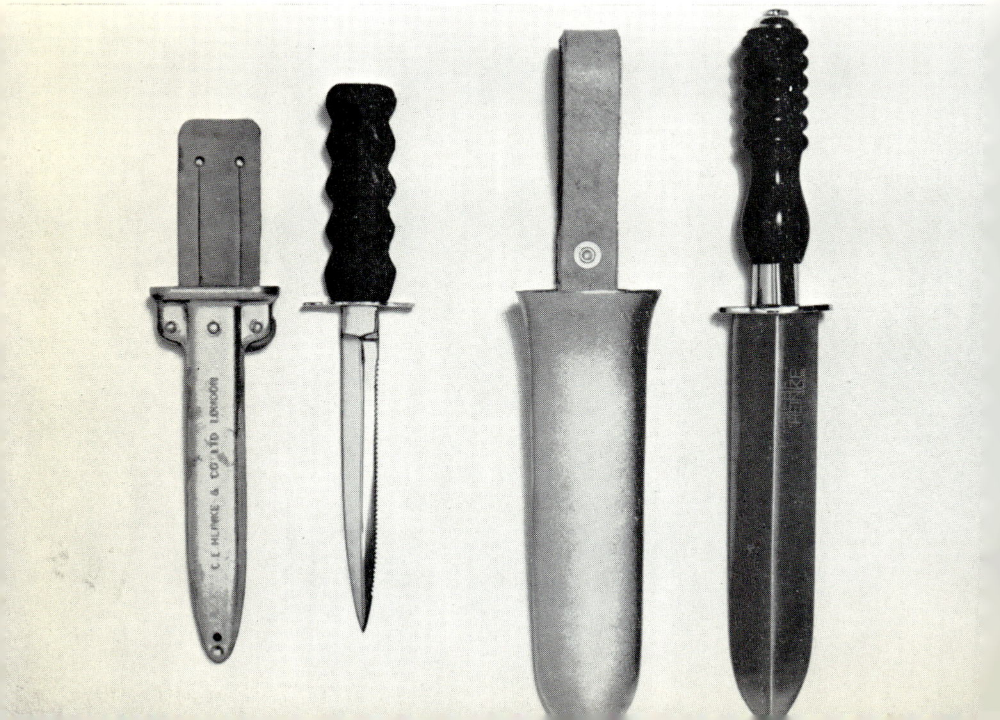

Page 90 (*above*) Standard diver boots with lead soles, 17 lb each; (*below*) left: frogman-type knife with metal sheath; right: heavy standard diver's knife with brass sheath

over the head. Without using finger-nails, but the pads of finger-tips, stretch the face aperture of the hood over the head and down round the neck. The top half can then be pulled down all round, until the top skirt covers the skirt on the trousers.

The diver then stands with legs apart, so that there is a nice tension on the two skirts. The two skirts are then rolled tightly together, working from the rubber bead on the bottom skirt, making very sure that no crease is allowed to form. A fold or crease will act as a tunnel up which water will easily penetrate.

A rubber cummerbund is then pulled up the legs and thighs, and stretched over the roll. The function of the cummerbund is merely that of holding the roll of skirts securely, so that they cannot unroll or slacken off. It is difficult to make a watertight roll on a thin person, and it may be necessary to pad them out under their woollen underclothing with a folded towel wrapped around their waist.

As the face aperture in the hood was designed to be covered by a full face mask, it is wise when using the ordinary aqualung type mouthpiece and face mask, to wrap a baby's napkin or towel around the neck. The rubber hood, although fitting tightly round the face, may allow a trickle of water to creep inside, and this is absorbed by the napkin. The hood is then carefully stretched over the head, the apparatus fitted, followed by the nose clip and mask, and the diver is ready for the descent.

If the diver is to remain dry, it is very necessary to remove the surplus air from the suit and underclothes by 'venting' efficiently. A neck seal in the suit is the amateur solution, but it makes venting difficult, dressing a struggle, and the trapped air in the underclothes cannot be used to prevent 'reverse ear'. On descending the ladder into the water, the arms are kept well down so that the air being forced out of the suit by external water pressure, cannot burst out of the cuffs, thereby letting water in. There is a rubber spear valve on the back of the hood through which the air can escape without ingress of water. When the shoulders are level with the water, the diver hesitates, allowing the bulk of the air to escape from the suit. Then, with the head bent forward, he descends into the water. This ensures that the outlet spear valve is the last part of the suited-diver to enter the water. If the head is held back, the last of the trapped air escapes out of the face aperture, letting in a lot of water.

A lot of air will still be squeezed out of the woollen underclothing as the pressure increases, so it is wise to descend down a shot rope to the working depth feet first, and looking down rather than up. Return to the surface for final ballast trimming. The next descent can be the more easily executed head-first swimming descent. A head-first descent with air in the suit, merely traps the air in the feet, which not only makes swimming difficult, but on starting to swim upwards again, the trapped air rushes to the top of the suit, and much of it escapes from the face aperture, again allowing the water to get in.

This type of suit, having a tight fitting hood, does not allow the external pressure of water to register on the ear-drum, and as the diver is breathing air at water pressure, his ear-drums will eventually burst outwards on a deep descent. They are therefore known as shallow water suits. This condition is known as 'reverse ear', and it can be circumvented by using a technique developed at the British Underwater Centre many years ago.

If, or when, a sharp pain becomes evident during descent, it is either due to a blocked eustachian tube or 'reverse ear'. The drill is to ascend immediately to a level at which the pain disappears, then clear eustachian tubes by blowing gently against the nose clip, or by pressing the mask up against the nostrils, then continue the descent. If the pain returns with the eustachian tubes cleared, then the pain is most likely due to 'reverse ear'.

Care should now be taken not to blow strongly against the closed nose, as the extra pressure may well rupture the ear-drum. Ascend again until the pain has gone, then make a feet first descent. The air trapped in the heavy diver's woollens is then squeezed out by the increasing pressure and, being lighter than water, moves up into the hood. This extra air in contact with the ear-drum, being at ambient pressure, allows a true balance of pressures on each side of the ear-drum.

As a dry suited diver will always lose buoyancy the deeper he goes, he must leave the surface with such a positive buoyancy that his buoyancy will be neutral at his working depth. On deep descents this will necessitate the use of a shot rope, as he will be too buoyant in the early stages to swim down, making the feet-first descent most convenient.

EAR PRESSURE COMPENSATORS

To overcome the problem of 'reverse ear' the writer designed the BUC Ear Pressure Compensator Cups, which were manufactured by C. E. Heinke & Co Ltd and issued with the following instructions:

> Ear Pressure Compensators are essential, both for comfort and safety, when making descents underwater with the head encased in airless, frogman-type rubber hoods. They are also very desirable when naked diving, as they prevent entry of water into the outer ear, always unpleasant and a source of infection, and yet they allow the true hydrostatic pressure to register on the outside of the ear-drum.
> Provided the eustachian tubes are cleared by exhaling against a nose-clip or by swallowing, etc, a balance of pressure is obtained on either side of the ear-drum, avoiding pain and ultimate rupture of the ear-drum.
> The design is such that the compression ratio will allow descents in excess of 100 ft to be made.
> The use of Ear Pressure Compensators also removes the very great danger, when wearing the hood over the ears, of trapping relatively high-pressure air outside the ear-drum on ascent. This is important, as, whilst a descent can be terminated, it is not always possible to delay an ascent due to shortage of air supply, or 'oxygen want' when skin diving.
> The carefully designed suction seal promotes an airtight joint around the ear, which ensures ambient pressure on the outside of the ear-drum. Any leakage from the reservoir of air can only occur after the desired balance has been obtained.

To increase the efficiency of the suction seal, a light frame is supplied which seats snugly around the rubber dome, and an adjustable rubber band passes over the top of the head, over the frames and under the chin. This rubber band also helps to keep the hood watertight. Tightening of the band will ensure a good seal, but long hair around the ears will make the seal more difficult to obtain.

Fitting

When fitting pressure compensators to frogman-type hoods,

mark position of ears carefully and cut out neatly a circular hole of 3-in diameter. Lightly roughen the hood and pressure compensator flange with glasspaper, then apply two coats of rubber solution thinly on hood and flange. Allow each coat to dry completely. Carefully insert the pressure compensator into the hole from the inside of the hood and press solutioned faces firmly together. Care is required when fitting to prevent hood tearing.

Note: As wet rubber solution causes the thin latex rubber to expand, failure to wait until the solution is quite dry before fitting hood to flange will result in the hole being too large and ugly creases will form.

Warning

When in use, any undue pressure on the rubber dome, such as heavy finger pressure when testing for leaks, will simulate a very rapid descent and can easily strain the delicate ear-drum. THEY ARE DESIGNED TO PROTECT YOUR EARS, SO DON'T MISUSE THEM.

With compensator cups fitted to the hood of a dry suit, the free-diver makes a normal descent until the ears give trouble. At the slightest sign of pain stop immediately and feel the compensators. They are bound to have collapsed to some extent, as this is a feature of the design, but if they are still 'squashy' in the smallest degree, any pain must be due to uncleared eustachion tubes, and the normal drill must be carried out. If the cups are pressed rigidly to the ears with sharp edges, then the diver has reached their limit, or the air in them has leaked out as a result of hair, or an unfortunate shaped bony structure around the ears, spoiling the seal, and the suit must then be treated the same as one not fitted with compensators. If the air has leaked out, it is certain that it will be able to leak in again on making a feet first descent, so nothing is lost.

If the diver happened to have a bad cold or catarrh, so that the increasing pressure could not reach his inner ear, then, of course, the rubber hood would help by holding back some of the external pressure. However, it is not a practice to be recommended as the eustachian tubes may suddenly clear at depth and the ear-drums would probably burst outwards.

* * *

Protective Clothing

The author has used shallow water diving suits down to 150 ft by reversing the usual arrangement of the full face mask over the hood aperture, and putting the mask on first and pulling the rubber hood over everything, so that the mask protrudes through the hood, the rubber of the hood making a nice seal on the smooth rubber of the full face mask. On descent, when the ears begin to hurt, instead of exhaling back into the mouthpiece, the air is exhaled out of the corner of the mouth and into the mask. This air then passes under the rubber of the mask and into the hood and reaches the outer ear-drum.

With a tight fitting hood, although unusual, ear-pain can sometimes occur on the ascent. This is due to the internal air pressure decreasing, and the hood trapping some relatively high pressure air on the outside of the ear-drum. Disturbing the hood around the affected ear with the hand will usually release the trapped air. Of course, it may be that the eustachian tubes are not clearing inwards, but this is rare owing to the normal shape of the tubes allowing pressure to be cleared easily in that direction.

Coarse woollen underclothing or string vests should not be worn under diving suits, except in very shallow water, as the pressure can badly bruise the skin and leave the pattern on the diver for days. The painful nip of clothing under pressure, between the legs and under the arms, can be the limiting factor when deep diving in dry protective swim suits.

Two-piece suits should have the braces detachable at the front, as a diver on the surface with further work ahead of him, has to remove the top half of the suit completely if nature calls. But without the braces, it is only necessary to unroll the skirts. Siebe, Gorman supply an unscrewing plate which can be fitted to all types of suits and dresses, but they look much too rude for most of us.

The one-piece frogman swim suit as used in the Royal Navy has the disadvantage that a dresser is necessary, whereas two-piece suits can be put on unaided. There is little room for underclothes and socks, but a thin nylon under-suit is supplied. The suit has a neck entry of only 4-in diameter, which has to be stretched so that it can be pulled up round the diver.

The diver stands up in the legs, and a dresser stands on either side of him, with one of their feet against his feet. With the palms of their hands well inside the rubber collar, to distribute the load, pulling outwards, they slip the suit up to the diver's neck. A channel section brass ring is then fitted inside the rubber collar, and a rubber hood is pulled over the head and stretched over the rubber neck of the suit and the neck ring. A brass strap is then placed round the joint and clamped up tightly.

This type of suit, used with a separate mask and mouthpiece, often leaves the diver with a wet patch down his chest. This may be because the rigid brass ring around the neck does not allow an efficient venting of air from the suit. A full-face mask covering the whole of the face aperture seems to be the only solution. Correctly used, a dry suit is dry, and pupils at the British Underwater Centre are trained to dive in their working clothes, on top of which are worn heavy diver's woollens.

REPAIRS

Swimsuits having the twill on the outside, seem to stand up to sunlight much better than suits having the rubber on the outside. The cuffs, skirts and hoods can be replaced quite easily when torn or perished. Repairs can be carried out to the lighter suits with cycle inner tube mending patches and solution, but before attempting a repair, the salt must be scrubbed out with soap and fresh water. Small holes can be invisibly repaired by patching on the inside, having roughened the rubber first. External rubber suits will have to be patched on the outside. Several layers of solution must be allowed to dry in turn before pressing down the prepared patching material.

In the case of standard diving dresses, the multi-ply twill material requires more serious treatment. A tear will require well washing and drying. Naphtha or unleaded petrol is applied round the damaged dress very sparingly, so that it does not affect the area of dress which is not to be patched. The twill material is then stripped off, exposing a layer of rubber $\frac{1}{2}$ in around the damage. An area extending 2 in around the damage is then solutioned and allowed to dry, several times. The prepared patch is then pressed down firmly, and it may, with advantage, be ironed with a warm iron, but not a hot one. The dress is then reversed and without stripping off the twill, another

Protective Clothing

patch is applied on the inside. A leaky seam can sometimes be repaired by rubbing in rubber solution and allowing to dry, once or twice.

Inserting new cuffs, collars, hoods, etc, is quite possible, but it is easy to bungle the job until experienced. The strips of tape covering the joints are removed by careful softening of the rubber with applications of naphtha or unleaded petrol, the damaged hood or cuff then being carefully removed.

The arm or neck of the suit is then drawn on to a tapered mandrel or a similar object of suitable size. In the case of a hood, a small bucket is excellent. The new rubber cuff or hood is then drawn on so that it overlaps the suit. A rubber band or string is then bound round the rubber at a point level with the suit underneath. The rubber is then turned back over the band and solutioned. The uncovered portion of the suit is also solutioned and both allowed to dry. This operation is repeated twice. Then when ready to stick together, the rubber is flicked over neatly on to the suit, and the two prepared surfaces pressed firmly together all round. The band or string is removed, the joint re-solutioned, and taped over on each side, using the original strips if not damaged on removal. The swim suit or diving dress is then ready for immediate use.

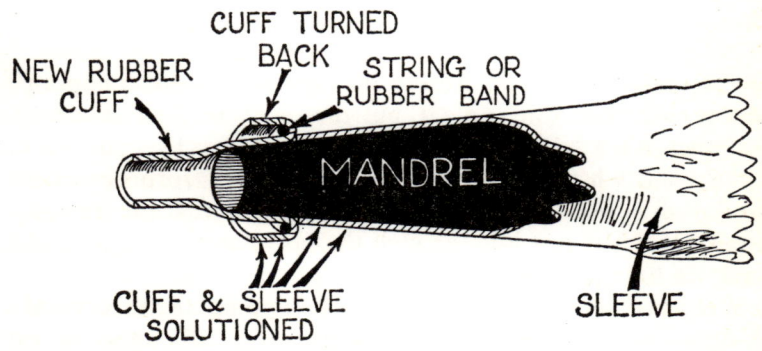

Inserting new cuff

Cleanliness of the parts to be repaired is achieved by slightly roughening the rubber surface with fine emery or glass paper and then rubbing this area with a petrol-damped, not wet, cloth.

The petrol-cleaned parts must dry before applying solution. Leave rubber surfaces, five minutes, fabric surfaces for fifteen minutes. A thin smear of solution over the surface is sufficient to make a good joint, but it must be a complete unbroken film. The solution must be nearly dry before the parts are brought together. Dampness of the solution is fatal to repair. After solutioning, the surfaces must be allowed to dry—rubber for fifteen minutes, and fabric for thirty minutes. Properly applied pressure will exclude all air blisters from a repair, thus permitting the full surfaces to bond together and prevent edges from being rubbed up.

It is an advantage to cut all patch material with a bevelled edge. This is accomplished by keeping the scissors almost flat in relation to the material. When patching a tear, press well down in position and use roller, then turn suit inside out and roll the patched area from the other side. Also, when replacing skirts, cuffs or hoods, roll the joint well, and after taping over seams roll the tape well into the seam line.

After use in salt water, all swim-suits and diving dresses should be washed down in fresh water. No material will dry completely with salt present. Salt, being hygroscopic, will absorb moisture out of the atmosphere, resulting in a permanent degree of dampness. These conditions will rot any fabric in time.

* * *

For underwater sport during the summer months, a sponge neoprene rubber suit is ideal, but the secret of their success is that they must be tight fitting round the arms, legs and neck. The sponge which has air trapped in the pores, forms excellent insulation between the body and the cold water. If the free passage of water is possible through the neck, arms or legs, it is a waste of time putting it on.

Wet suits have the advantage of not 'nipping' the divers body on deep descents, but some of them are more difficult to put on than a well designed dry suit, and the necessary undressing and getting wet limits their appeal to the sporting diver. They are also acceptable to the inexpert diver, as no special techniques have to be learnt.

Other swim-suits are manufactured, having variations of designs and material. There are pure rubber suits with neck entry, back entry and front entry, some of them being tied up, others clamped up, and several with stiff rubber seals and gaskets which join at the neck or waist. All pure rubber creations tend to perish in sunlight. Metal zip fasteners are to be avoided, as they leak and soon give trouble under harsh sea-going conditions. There is certainly room for experiment in plastic and neoprene swim-suits, and possibly standard diving dresses.

A tight fitting heavy knitted woollen jumper is quite effective, providing water cannot flow past the body. A polo necked jumper with tight cuffs, a pair of shorts and a belt, make a very good sporting diving rig. The harness of breathing apparatus is always more comfortable with something underneath it.

Compressed air apparatus, of the open circuit type, refrigerates the air slightly, due to the expansion of the highly compressed air. This cold air absorbs a lot of body heat between inhalation and exhalation. The naked diver also loses heat rapidly by conduction. As the nervous system is mainly confined to the external body, the internal loss of heat is barely noticed, so the diver is inclined to stay in the water until the outer body becomes chilled. The breathing tube diver does the same, but he has the internal heat for his outer extremities to draw upon. The aqualung diver has less internal reserves and is in a worse condition. It is therefore wise to leave the water before becoming really chilled.

Cold water affects metabolism, increasing oxygen consumption and respiration. Fatigue and exhaustion result, with further loss of body heat. In these circumstances, exercise does not keep the diver warm, and heat is lost rapidly. The temperature of the body falls and the diver becomes light headed and hazy minded, eventually lapsing into unconsciousness. A naked aqualung diver often suffers from a bad attack of shivering after leaving the water, which he cannot understand, as he has not begun to feel cold externally. Nature obviously knows better, and promotes shivering to induce warmth.

The Admiralty Climatic Chart (Sheet No 2), shows for the month of July a 60-degree isotherm running just south of the Cornish and South Devon coast, through the Channel Islands and into Normandy. It is based on average sea temperature, so that individual days may be a little higher or lower, but the sea temperature varies little from day to day a mile or two offshore. The temperature gradient then falls steadily as one moves north, so that in the Western Isles of Scotland an isotherm would show an average sea temperature for the same month as 54 degrees. The January chart shows a similar isotherm gradient up the west coast, but a good 10 degrees lower.

Shallow waters inshore will vary more from day to day, and may become several degrees warmer during good weather, but these shallow waters are often river estuaries with reduced underwater visibility. Steep to rocky coasts have waters at more constant temperatures with a warm layer near the surface in quiet weather. A gale, however, will very quickly reduce the surface temperature to the average for the month of the year.

The 70-degree isotherm runs from the latitude of Washington, through the Azores to Madeira and the Canary Islands. The 80-degree isotherm runs from Charleston, north of the West Indian Islands, half-way across the Atlantic, and then doubles back off the coast of South America to Panama, enclosing the West Indies and the Gulf of Mexico in a delightful warm pocket of water, denied to the coast of Africa or South America.

The Mediterranean can only claim an average water temperature between 65–70 degrees. The hottest sea water in the world is found in the Persian Gulf, where, for the month of July, the temperature reaches 96 degrees, with the Red Sea only 2 degrees lower.

The inshore sea water temperature of Devon and Cornwall can rise to 65 degrees, and only drops to 40 degrees for a week or two during February. Most of the winter it is above 45 degrees, and up to Christmas it is usually well over 50 degrees.

10
FISHES AND CRUSTACEA

WHILST the author cannot claim to be a very enthusiastic underwater fisherman, he has caught fish, lobsters and crabs using various underwater apparatus. As he only fishes for food or the value of the fish, he finds nets, long-line and pots much more lethal.

Due to quite different conditions existing in sub-tropical and tropical waters, a lot of nonsense is talked about control and the restriction of underwater fishing around the coasts of the United Kingdom. As a professional inshore fisherman of several years standing the author advocates unrestricted freedom for underwater fishermen, whether using breathing apparatus or not.

As regards other parts of the world where local fishermen claim that their fishing grounds have been fished out, it is much more likely that the fish moved off when their haunts were invaded by numerous 'menfish'. In a small way, this has happened in Devon in particular areas where training has been in progress day after day, and with not a shot fired.

However, the important point is that in warmer latitudes the local fishermen depend on the inshore fish as their means of livelihood. In our northern seas our offshore waters are teeming with first class edible fish that are trawled, seined, and long-lined in millions upon millions. Nobody cares a 'tinker's cuss' about the inshore rockfish, which is all that underwater swimmers are likely to frighten off. The idea of 'fishing out' the wrasse, pollack, mullet, etc is ludicrous to anyone with the least knowledge of marine biology. Life under the sea has so many hazards for its fishy denizens, that it would need half the nation hunting underwater to make a fraction of 1 per cent difference to the overall balance of nature in our coastal waters.

The real danger to our supplies of edible fish is the damage wreaked in the breeding grounds by the deep sea trawlers, so that billions of fish are destroyed before they leave the egg stage. When one considers the magnitude of the world's fishing and whaling industries, the concern about a few harpoon guns and spears in the hands of aqualung divers creating havoc is quite misplaced.

As regards unnecessary killing from a humane point of view, the author must admit that he has returned many a fish to the sea unharmed, but it is purely a personal whim. We must be realistic about the killing of fish, and appreciate that a natural death in the ocean is anything but dying at a ripe old age. Any fate that we may mete out to our fishy adversary can only be as kind or kinder than the one nature has in store for him. To be eaten or digested alive, is as much as he can expect.

Regarding sportsmanship—man coined the word, not nature. The fish also has a breathing apparatus, and it is better than an aqualung. He has no harpoon gun, but on the other hand he has by far the superior performance. He may not have your monkey cunning, but then with his lower intelligence, he will not suffer the mental agonies that you will when the 'chop' comes. If you want him to eat or sell, go for him with a jet propelled aqualung and an atomic harpoon gun if necessary, but if not, live and let live, in the hopes that his big brother will hear of your magnanimity.

LOBSTERS

In America they have controlled the catching of lobsters, and only allow the underwater hunter so many per day. There is certainly no case for restricting the catch of lobsters by underwater methods until we have also been stopped hooking them out of their holes at low water, during the August spring tides. The back of a car has been filled with them in a morning. Lobsters come inshore during August for the protection of the rocks while they cast their shells and their new ones are hardening. Every lobster caught underwater using expensive breathing apparatus, physical energy, and not a little courage, has been well earned, and no reasonable person will begrudge the underwater fisherman his catch. The fishermen of Brittany catch their lobsters in nets, often 7 miles long. They can be seen unloading them off San Servain in the river Rance, fifty baskets at a time, with fifty lobsters in each basket.

We must not allow possibly well meaning but misinformed individuals to stampede a government department into making more quite unnecessary controls. It may be that they hope to be given the task of issuing licences, and so get control of a sport which certainly does not need controlling.

When tackling a lobster underwater in the open, keep his attention attracted with one hand, whilst the other hand is brought up behind him. Grab him round the body, close up to where his large claws join the body. Then providing he is held away from the face, he can do little harm. If he is approached from his front, when reached for he will shoot off backwards, very rapidly for a short distance. Very often a second approach can be made, resulting in a catch, if a little cunning is practised. They seem to be more puzzled than alarmed. A lobster with his back to a rock or lobster pot, can be caught by the same method, but you have to pounce on him from above.

During daylight they are usually to be found amongst the rocks or under the remains of wrecks. Most of them are holed up with only their antennae showing. It is a mistake to try and handle them in this position, although it can be done by experts, for a nasty nip is likely to result. Even rubber gloves will not protect you from a large lobster. If you are nipped and he does not let go, jerk your hand, and he will probably shed the claw. A lobster will often nip and then let go, but an edible crab will nip and hang on.

At a conference held by the Ministry of Agriculture, Fisheries and Food in December 1958, which was attended by representatives of the British Underwater Centre, the Birmingham Underwater Explorers Club, the Looe Underwater Club, and the British Sub Aqua Club, it was decided that there was no case for banning underwater fishing, with or without breathing apparatus, but it was agreed that clubs should advise their members to refrain from using tools or weapons in the catching of shell fish. To be safe for eating, crabs and lobsters need to be alive until ready for the cooking pot, so that damaging them with spears, etc can render them useless, and naturally infuriates the local fishermen.

CRABS

A large edible crab, often found in the open in deep water, can be approached from behind. He will require two hands to hold him securely, each hand round the arms of his claws. A medium sized crab can be held in one hand with the palm of the hand down his back, the wrist being at his head, and the fingers tucked round his tail. If he does get hold of you, smash him up quickly. Even then his claw might hold on for some time.

The amount of meat in lobsters and crabs varies considerably. A crab that has leg joints showing yellow through the thin skin, will always be full of good meat. The female edible crab can be identified by its wide egg pouch or apron, underneath, sometimes filled with bright orange-coloured eggs.

The edible crab is not the only crab that is edible. Spider crabs are edible and very nice but in Britain it is the custom to eat only the legs. The swimming, or lady crab, is also good eating. It can be identified by its smooth velvet body and flat, back swimming legs. They never grow very large, but they are as nice to eat as lobsters. Their legs are soft, and the meat can be squeezed straight into the mouth, as you squeeze tooth-paste out of a tube.

UNDERWATER FISHING

For the underwater fisherman, the south and west coasts of the British Isles offer reasonable sport, but we cannot claim that it is as good, or should we say as easy, as in some parts of the world.

A spear with a three-pronged trident can be made up quickly and easily. A cane with the spear end cut off through one of the joints and three straightened out cod hooks seized on with a strong whipping of copper wire, can be most effective in securing rock fish and flat fish.

Providing a fish is approached quietly, it is easy to get within range, but any sudden movement will make it apprehensive and it will keep out of range. Chasing fish is a waste of time, for once

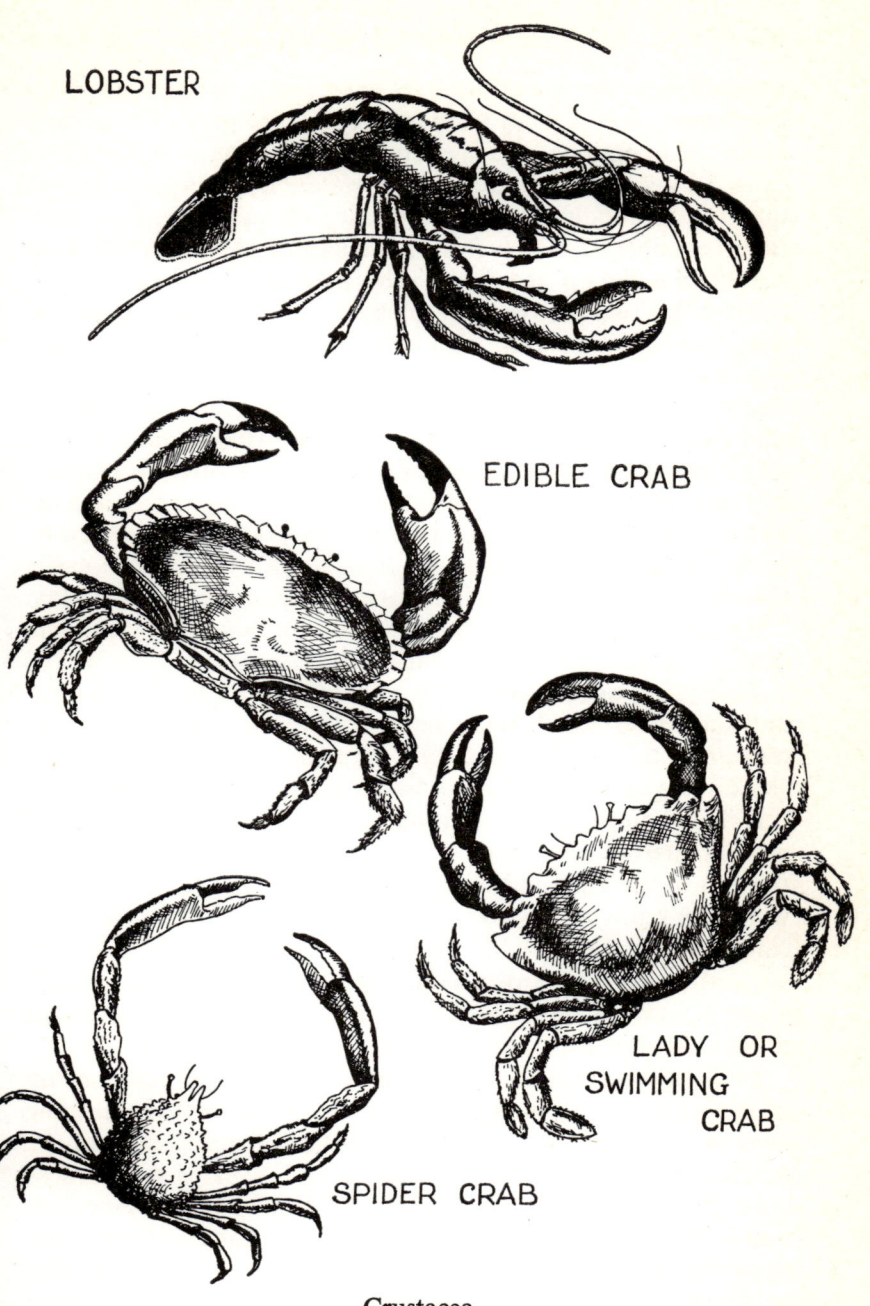

Crustacea

alarmed they slide off effortlessly much faster than a swim-diver can hope to travel. They seem to have a sense which warns them of hostile intentions, and they undoubtedly react to shock waves caused by violent agitation of the water. By approaching very quietly, and holding the breath if using an aqualung, it is sometimes possible to take a fish in the hands. However, the diver would go hungry if he relied on this method of capture.

There are two sizes of harpoon gun available. The smaller one is of toylike dimensions, with a frail looking harpoon having a multi-pronged head on it. This is a useful gun for the average rockfish around the coast, and is excellent for flat fish. The harpoon is attached to the gun by a short line, which is looped back and held by a spring clip until fired. For very obvious reasons, it is dangerous to use harpoon guns having a range exceeding the water visibility. The larger pattern of harpoon gun powered by spring, compressed air, and single or double elastic, can easily transfix a man, and they often have a range exceeding visibility. They are intended for use against fish exceeding 5 lb, and will deal with tope, skate, small shark, etc.

These guns usually have a nylon harpoon line 20 or 30 ft long, and sometimes a reel. When ready to fire, the reel must have its tensioning device slackened right off, and a bight of line hanging slack from the gun. This allows the harpoon to start on its travels unhampered. Other models have a catch on the stock, which collapses on squeezing the trigger. The line is secured to the end of the gun, and brought back over the catch, then forward to a knob on the front of the gun, and back again over the catch until all the slack has been taken up. The loose end is then secured to the harpoon traveller, and the gun is ready to load. Guns must not be left loaded out of the water, neither should the diver unload by firing into the water from the surface.

In Britain there is some confusion regarding the relationship of harpoon guns to the Gun Licence and Firearm Act, and the local ruling should be obtained from the police authority of the district in which the user is operating.

In shooting with a harpoon gun, little accuracy is expected, and it is difficult to hit a 5-lb fish at 10-ft distance. On the final approach, stop breathing when using compressed air apparatus, as some species of fish dislike the bubble stream. Much larger

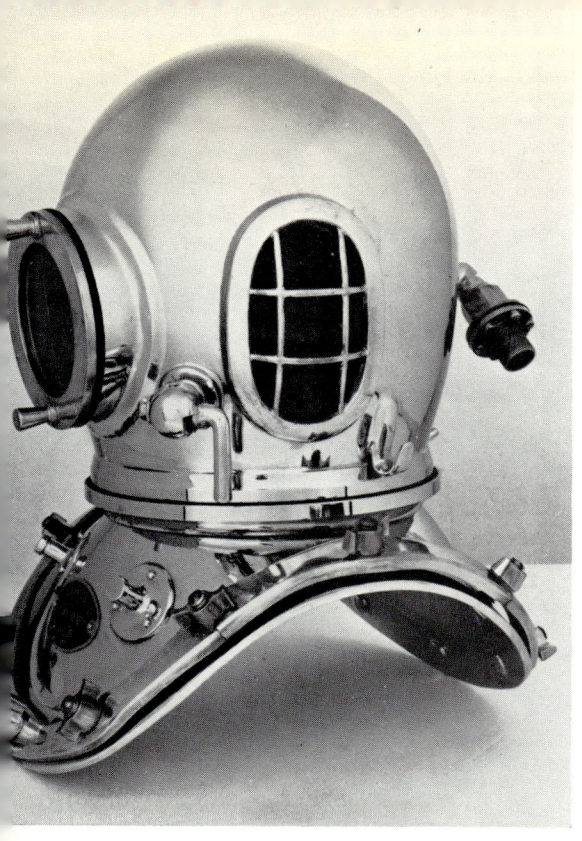

Page 107 (*above*) Helmet and twelve-bolt corselet; (*below*) two-diver mobile compressor unit, complete with divers' panel, filters and air receiver

Page 108 (*above*) Admiralty pattern twin-cyclinder handpump for two divers in shallow water (40 ft), or one diver in deep water (90 ft); (*below*) HP reducing valve for surface supply demand valve apparatus

catches of mullet and bass have been caught off the south coast, using only breathing tubes, but this may have been due to the greater experience of the hunter. Twelve nice bass of several pounds each have been brought to the surface within an hour, by the same diver.

Probably our best underwater game fish is the bass, which goes to 20 lb, 12-lb bass being quite common. They are cunning and unpredictable in their habits and abound along the south coast and up to the west coast of England and Wales. They are of the perch family, having spined dorsal fins. Their colour is bluish on the back, with silver sides, white underparts and large scales. In rough weather and during the winter months they are inclined to go deep. They are shy and will leave an area in which there is constant activity. They are very good to eat, especially baked and stuffed.

Wrasse are the most common rock fish around our shores, growing to approximately 8 lb. Their colour and markings vary considerably and they really are the most beautiful fish. They range between green, brown and red, with lovely variation of these colours. Sometimes they will swim alongside a diver or peer inquisitively through his face mask. Their flesh is said to be tasteless, and they are not usually eaten in Britain, but some Channel Islanders consider them a great delicacy stuffed. Occasionally they are caught up to 12 lb in weight.

Another prolific fish is the pouting, which frequents a rocky bottom, but it only grows to 2 lb or so. Big pollack, up to 20 lb, can be hunted off all the rocky coasts of Britain, but they are not acceptable in the kitchen. Rather than waste them, they can be made up into fish cakes, which are nice enough to justify their killing.

Grey mullet, which arrives in large numbers on the south and south-west coasts during the summer, is an excellent fish to hunt as it is very difficult to catch by any other method. It is found in estuaries, harbours, docks, etc and is quite good to eat.

Flatfish are found on all coasts on a sandy bottom. They have to be searched for, swimming just clear of the bottom. A spear or the smaller type of gun with a trident headed harpoon is perfect, as it enables the diver to search with his eyes closer to the bottom, with the gun at the ready. Only the eyes and perhaps a

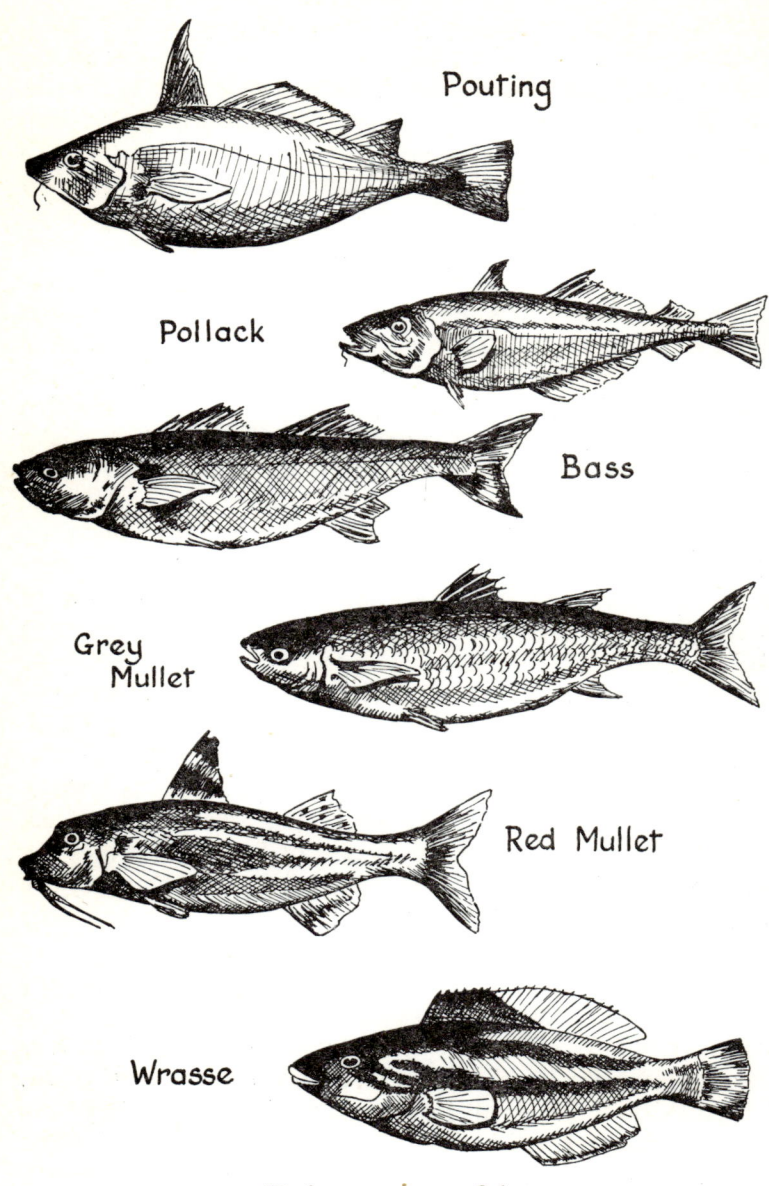

Underwater game fish

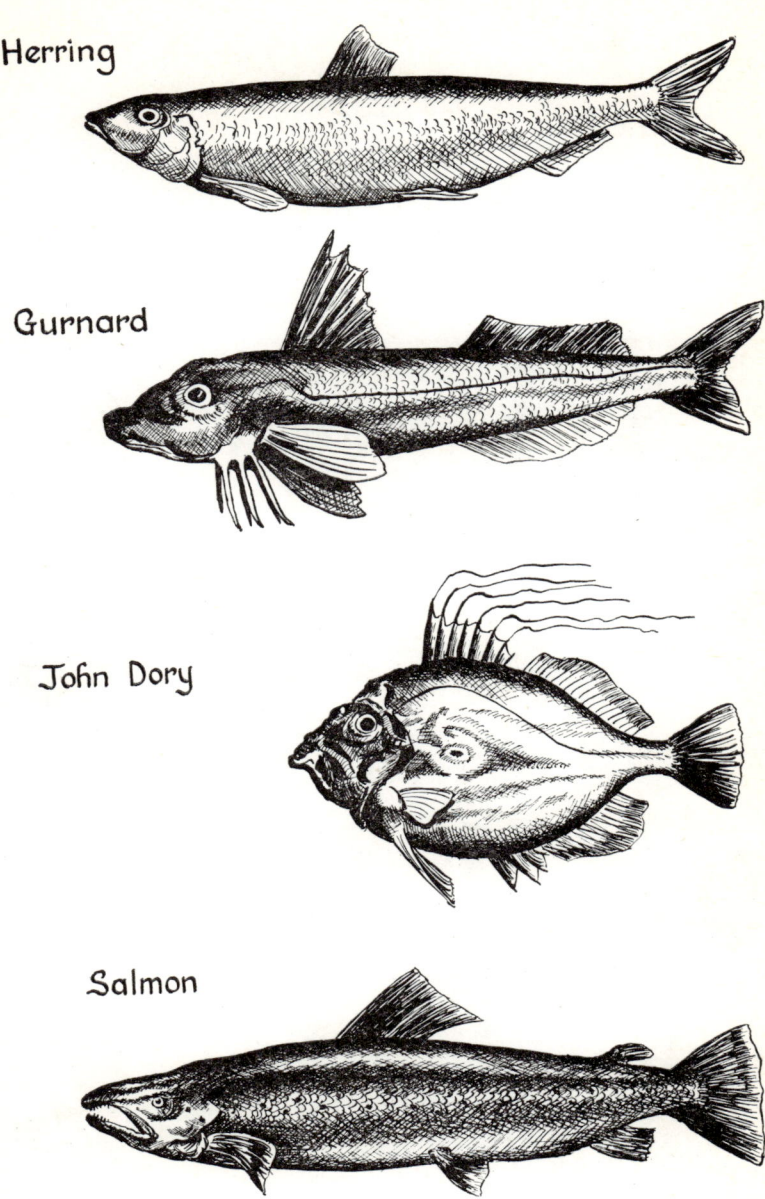

Underwater game fish

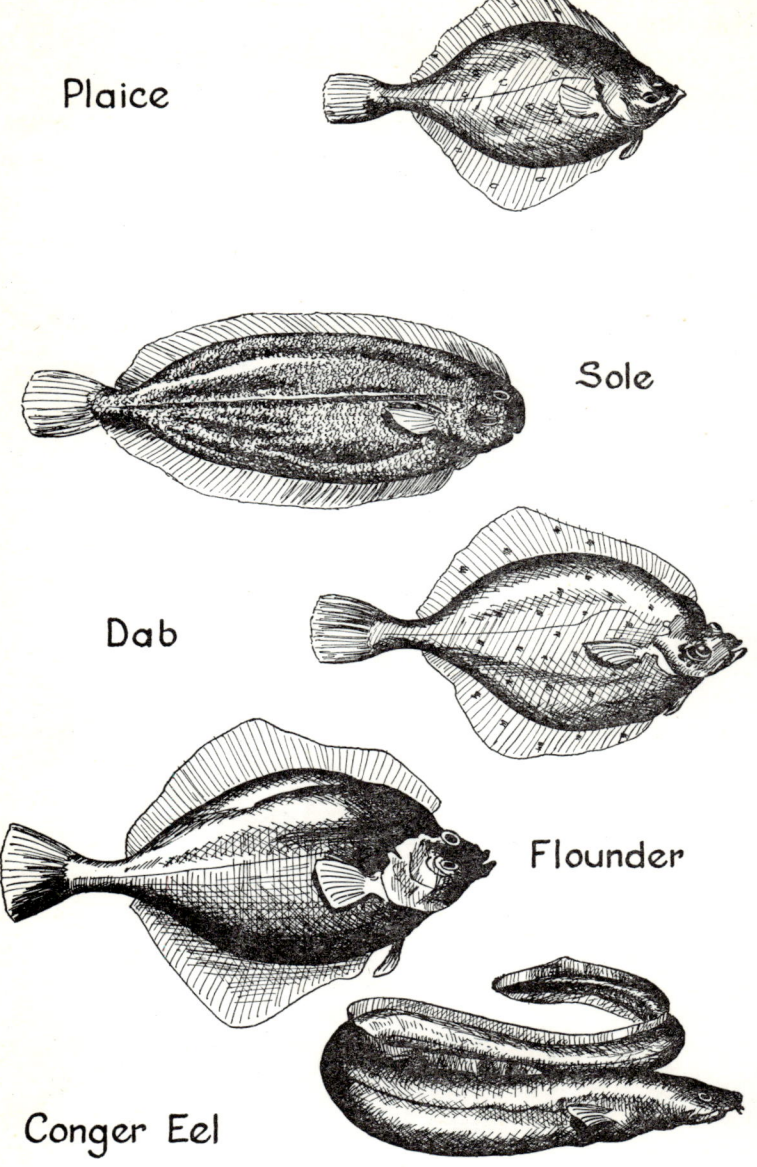

Underwater game fish

faint outline of the fish show above the sand. Fire on sight, for they move like lightening once they decide to go.

The common sole is a most sought after flatfish, but he is rarely seen by day. However, it is possible to catch him feeding occasionally in thick water. Having caught your sole, he must be skinned, and should really be kept for two days before eating. The lemon sole can be speared at 30 ft or deeper on a sandy bottom but they do not grow very large.

Plaice are found on nice clean sand, and in large numbers well off shore. Dabs and flounders can be found at anytime in the more accessible shallow waters on a bottom of mud and sand. The angler fish is also found on the bottom, usually stationary. A big one of 60 or 70 lb can look quite formidable. They have nasty teeth and an enormous mouth, which it is wise to keep clear of. The larger more powerful harpoon gun will be required for this customer.

Do not insert hands into dark holes, for apart from the nip of a lobster, you might find a conger. By day he lives in his lair amongst the rocks, and it is really best to leave him there. He takes a lot of killing and cannot be pulled out of his hole by brute force. If he does get hold of your hand, cut his head off with the knife you should always carry. If his head cannot be reached with the other hand, keep a steady pull with the trapped hand, then suddenly push the hand down his throat and whip it back in the same movement, the theory being that as your pull slackens, he relaxes his grip to get a better bite, giving you at least a small chance of withdrawing the hand whole. It might work—anyway it is nice to feel there is a plan of escape laid down.

It is the larger and much more romantic fish that our enthusiastic underwater hunters dream about, and it is generally imagined that they are only found in distant waters. It is true to a certain extent, but shark are widely distributed, and although more often seen in warmer waters, they do frequent all the seas of the world.

In home waters the blue shark and dogfish are fairly common. The blue shark is found off the west coast of Britain and around the Irish coast. Where the currents run strongly, they keep well down, but in slacker water they feed nearer the surface. Dogfish,

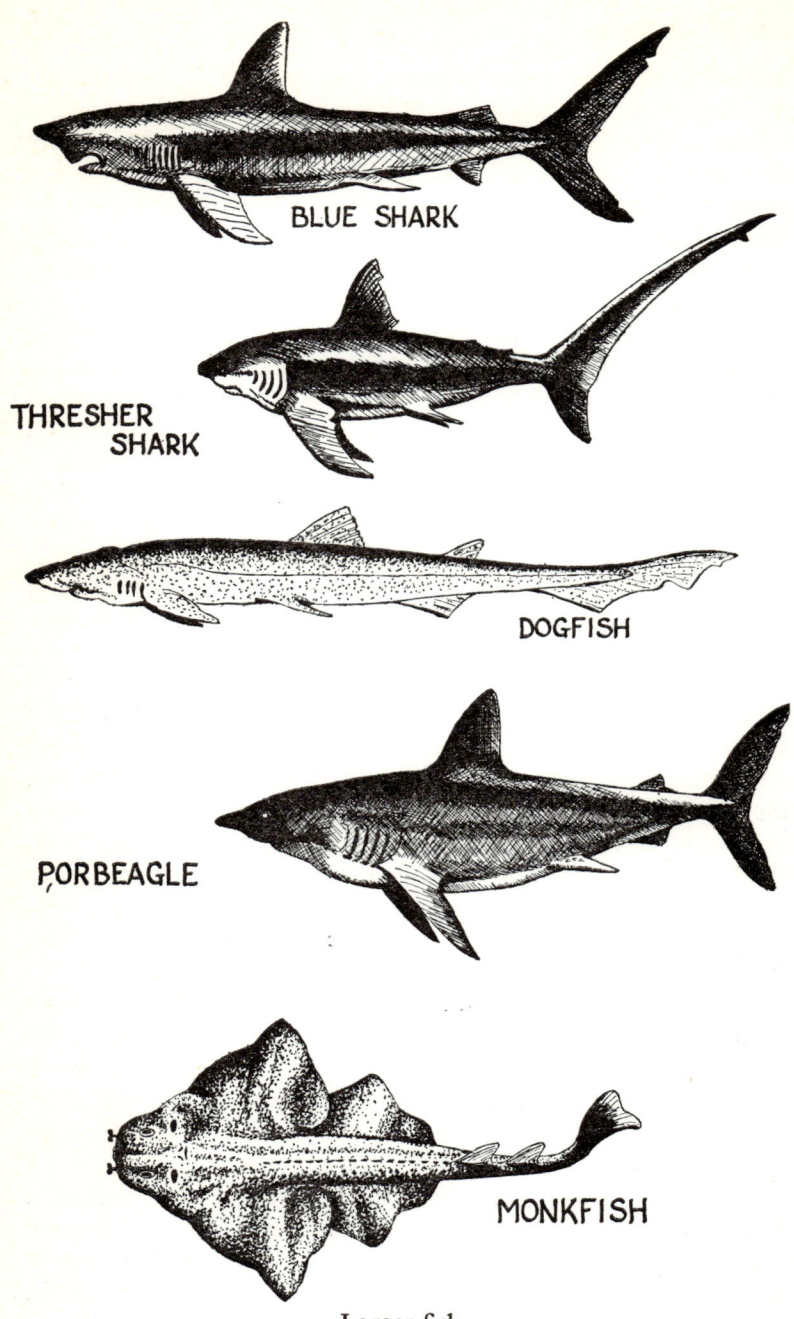

Larger fish

which is a species of shark, can be hunted in shallow water, and the lesser spotted dogfish is a good fish to eat. The flesh is clean and free of bones and makes very good fish cakes or fish pie. The thresher shark appears everywhere, and they have been seen off the Dorset coast by underwater hunters as well as further west. They can be recognised by their exceedingly long thin tail.

The monk fish is another of our larger fish, and although classed with sharks, looks more like a ray. Some people incorrectly call the angler fish a monk fish. Another really large fish found in home waters is the porbeagle, which runs to over 300 lb in weight, although 100 lb is more usual.

The well-known skate can be hunted on the same ground as flatfish, and although the large 200-lb specimens are found in deep water, 100-lb skate do occur off our beaches. Our local waters can even produce the sting ray, which is found all round the coast but is most numerous in the south. They have a long serrated sting rising from the tail, which can inflict a wound which will most likely become infected. A sting ray of over 50 lb has been caught in the Solent. Other rays likely to be seen are the spotted-ray, cuckoo-ray, sandy-ray which is common off South Devon and the bottlenose ray.

The bottlenose ray is thicker than most rays and its snout is very pointed. It is the largest British ray, and it is found in large numbers in the west Channel. Several caught have exceeded 500 lb, but the average ranges around 100 lb.

Other fish likely to be encountered by underwater hunters off our coasts are John Dorys off the Devon coast and herrings in the vicinity of harbour walls along the south coast during the early months of the year. The gurnard, although usually small, sometimes reaches a weight of 5 lb or more, and is then worth hunting. They are very good eating, but should be handled carefully as they have sharp spines, which although not poisonous, can be very painful. Many other fish will be encountered, as one of our underwater fishermen realised as he watched a magnificent salmon glide away unharmed—with the hunter spellbound.

Repeating earlier advice, if you require a fish, hunt him with avidity and enthusiasm, for despite your mechanical advantages it is still his environment and you are only one of the minor

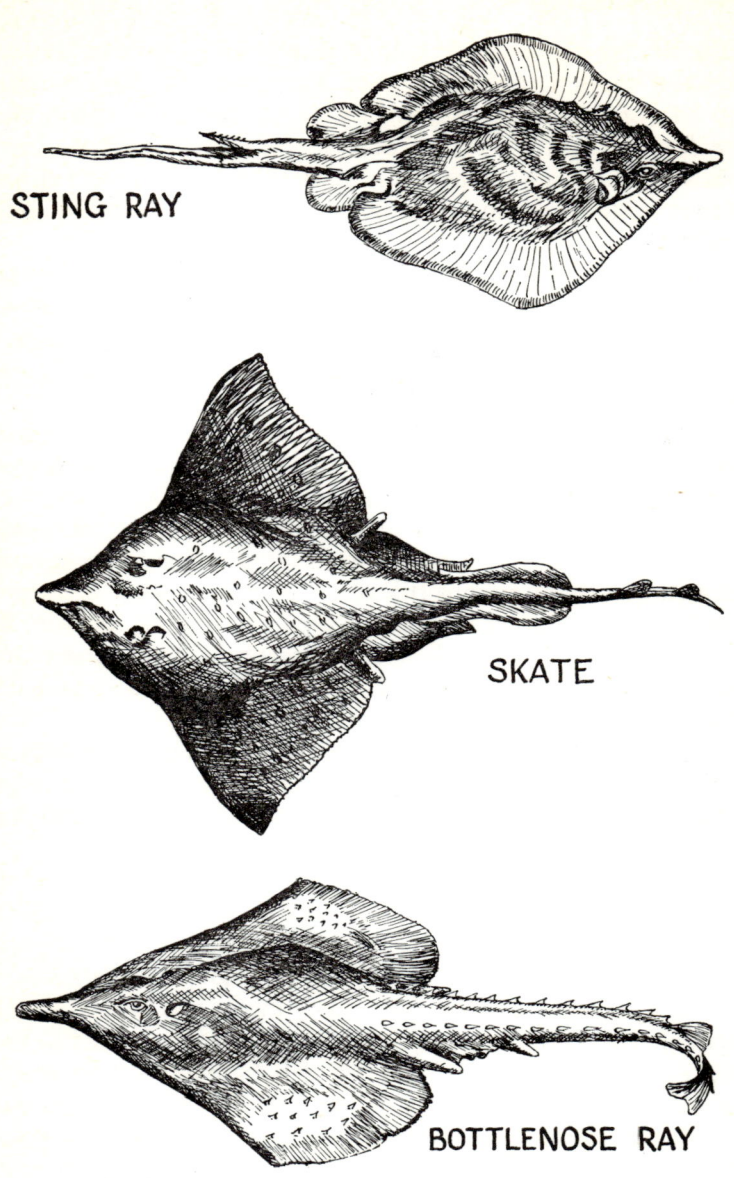

Skate and ray

dangers to his continued existence. If they have to die, they would prefer to die quickly with a minimum of pain. It is their predestination, come what may. It is even doubtful whether they experience our sort of pain, as pain is surely a product of imagination and intelligence. If you do not require their bodies, leave your harpoon gun in the boat, and allow them to survive a little longer.

When hunting in thick water, look out for trammel nets. They are cleverly designed to entangle fish in their folds, and a 'man-fish' would be no exception. If you drove into the net at speed, it might be a long, slow job cutting yourself out. Frantic struggling only entangles the victim more, and as the net is usually 120-ft long and weighted to the bottom, it might be serious. Cork buoys usually mark each end, but they could easily be mistaken for harmless lobster pots.

Do not remove lobsters or crabs from lobster pots. They have already been caught and it would be stealing of a high order. Offenders finish up in court. Even worse, you will lose the goodwill of the local fishermen and you may need their help one day.

If you would not consider harpooning a dog, you will not be tempted to attack a seal or porpoise for sport alone. The seal has a higher intelligence than any dog, and it would be a callous hunter that harms these exceedingly friendly creatures. They are most inquisitive and cannot resist a working diver. Their antics are really comic as they peer and twist their heads about in order to obtain a better view of what is going on.

11

THE SUBMARINE SEASCAPE

SEAWEEDS

Most of the rock in our coastal waters is covered with seaweeds consisting of three main groups, green, brown and red. The brown weeds predominate and include the wracks and kelps. The green and red weeds provide the beauty and the food. The most extensive of the green weeds is the sea lettuce, and it is easily distinguished by the broad flat fronds with wavy edges. It looks attractive and is actually edible. It is not the only seaweed that is edible. Purple-dulse, plamate-dulse and pepper-dulse have all been substance of food in earlier days, mainly in Scotland. Pepper-dulse is stewed and eaten with lemon juice.

An extensive green weed is gut-weed which has tubular green fronds and bubbles of gas at regular intervals. The red, purple and mauve weeds take several beautiful forms such as Irish moss, star moss, polysiphonia and coral-weed. Of the brown weeds the commonest is the bladder-wrack. This is the weed that has the delightful bubbles along it stem and fronds, which explode loudly when squeezed in the fingers.

Next in abundance are the many smooth fronded kelps that grow to such amazing lengths. There is the fingered-kelp, quite unmistakable, and the long wavy-edged fronds of sugared-kelp, together with furbelow or bulbous-kelp. Sugared-kelp is the seaweed taken home by holiday-makers, who have great faith in its weather forecasting properties. It can also feature in the production of saccharine. It grows to a great length, sometimes 20 ft long.

Fingered-kelp hangs from overhanging rocks in 4-ft curtains.

It makes excellent cover for the underwater hunter with his camera or harpoon gun. It is often behind this curtain of weed, in the clear space between the weed and the rock, that the larger fish take shelter during daylight. The breathing apparatus diver can push through the weeds to the tunnel formed round, and under, the overhanging rock. This underwater shelter gives the diver the same impression of comfort and safety that the lurking fish must feel, as he peers through the curtain at the outside watery world.

A weed which is quite a hindrance at times is the cord-weed, which grows 12 ft long and looks like round bootlaces. It is very strong and slippery, and free-divers often come up with it draped around their self-contained apparatus. Sausage-weed as its name implies, is round and divided off like a string of sausages.

There are many variations and sub-divisions of all these weeds, which together with the sponges, sea-anemones, star-fish and shell-fish form the background of a new and wonderful playground for those who dare. These wonders of the deep cry out to be photographed in their natural setting, so that some small part of submarine enchantment can be captured for those who dally ashore.

PHOTOGRAPHY

Underwater photography can play an important part in underwater sport and open sea salvage work, but in the more usual waters where underwater work is required, such as docks, canals, rivers, etc its usefulness is limited by visibility, which is never very great. Even under the best conditions off our coasts, we can hardly expect to get the same brilliant photographic results as our fortunate friends in the West Indies or even in the Mediterranean. As in surface photography, the worse the conditions, the better the camera required, and an expensive camera requires a well designed waterproof case, if finance is to be considered at all.

Camera cases can be manufactured in a variety of materials, including metals, plastics and rubber. There is not much point in working for extreme lightness, as displacement will have to be

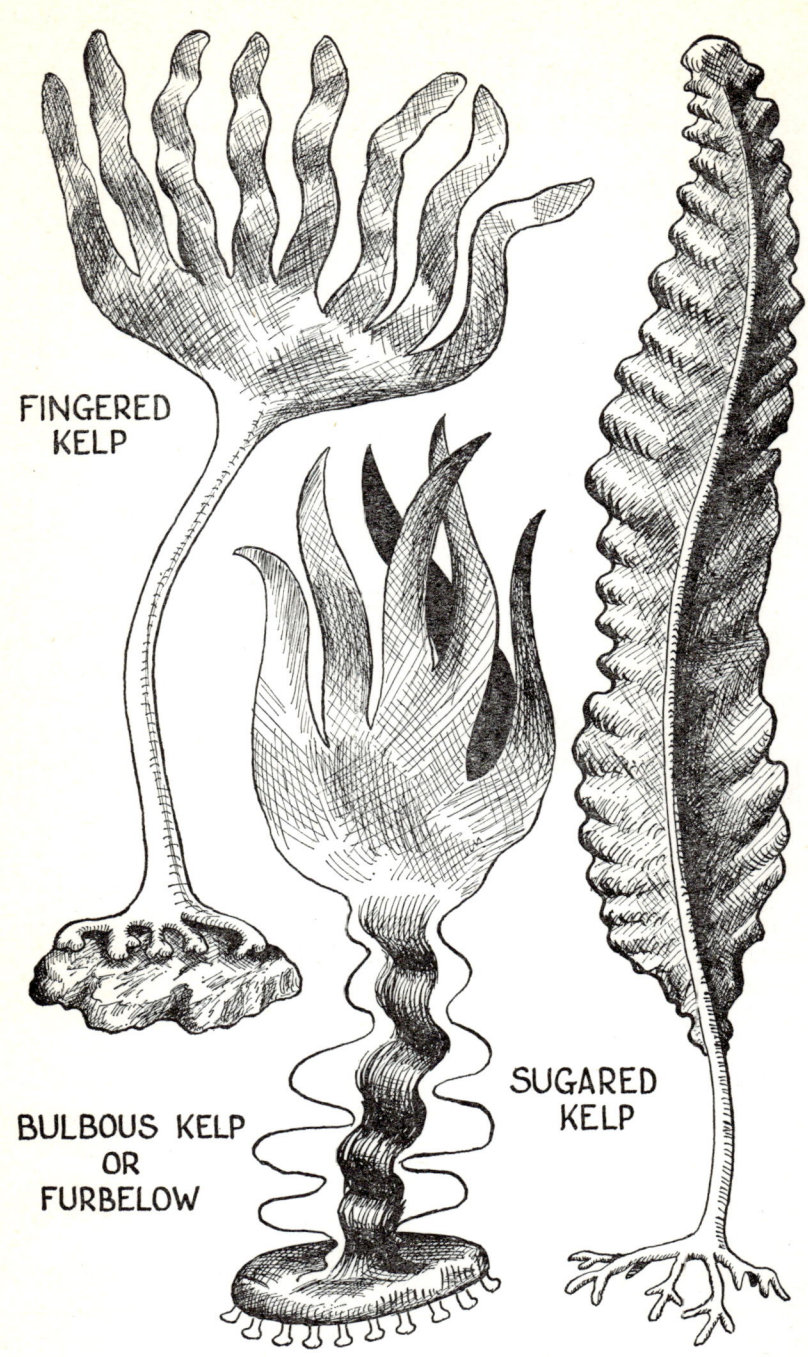

Common sea weeds

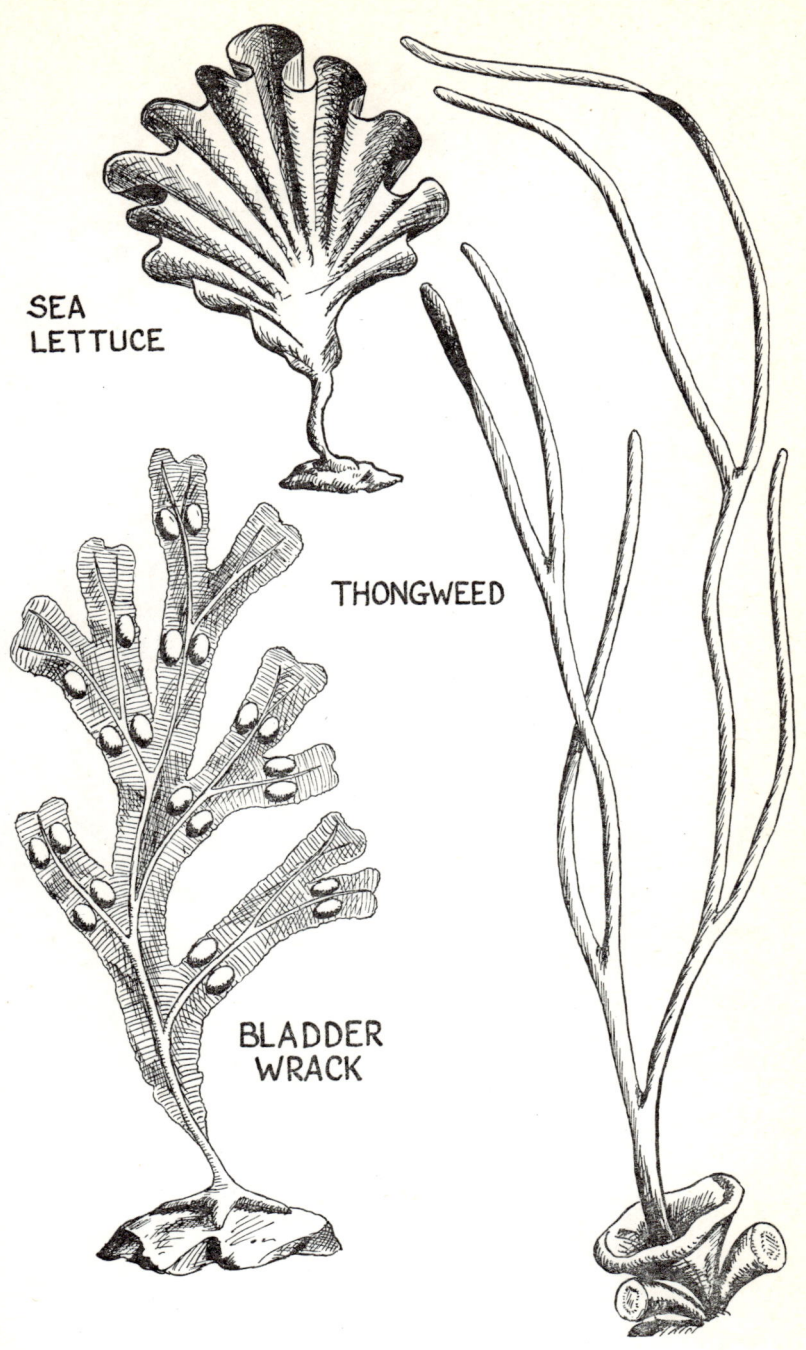

Common sea weeds

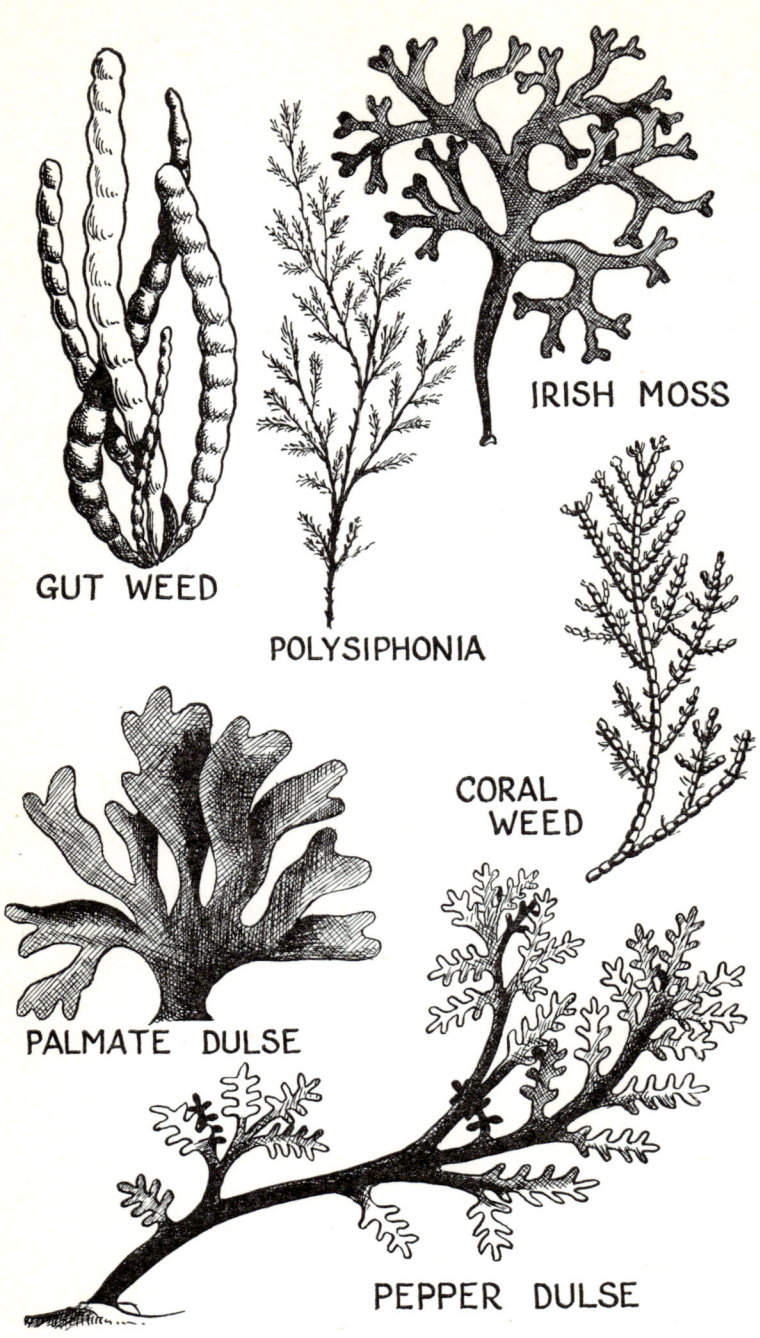

Common sea weeds

The Submarine Seascape

more or less ballasted out anyway. Every cubic inch of air inside the case will require ·6 oz of ballast, less the weight of the case and camera. A camera case 6 in × 4 in × 4 in will therefore have to weigh 57 oz or approximately $3\frac{1}{2}$ lb to give it a negative buoyancy.

Transparent perspex is easily worked and can be cemented with a solvent such as chloroform. Watertight glands must be engineered through which the remote control rods can operate the shutter release, wind on, focussing, and if possible, the stop and speed controls. If the case is not to be pressurised, all movements must be rotational rather than reciprocal, as the latter operate themselves prematurely as the external water pressure increases. A perspex case has the great advantage that any entry of water can be seen by the diver, and he can surface before the camera is flooded.

One form of camera case consists of a cylinder of perspex with one end left open. The camera is mounted inside with the lens near the flat perspex end of the cylinder. The open end of the cylinder has a surgical rubber glove stretched over it and secured so that it is watertight. The glove is then pushed inside out, up the cylinder with the hand inside the glove. The hand is then in a position to hold the camera and operate the controls, and the air inside the glove and the cylinder has been compressed to some small extent. The camera can then be used around the two atmosphere pressure level of 33 ft. This design has the disadvantage that the case must be large enough to insert the hand, which results in bulkiness and unnecessary buoyancy.

With a cheap camera, chances can be taken with thin rubberised waterproofing. For instance a face-mask glass and clamping strap can be fitted to the end of a section of a car inner-tube. The camera is inserted, and the open end doubled over and clamped with two strips of brass bolted together with wing nuts and bolts. It will have its disadvantages, as you will find when you feel for the controls, but it will work. A football bladder, being thinner, will allow more positive feel of the controls, but the face-mask clamping strap will be the only means of entry. Specially designed underwater cameras needing no case are also available.

The diver notices that objects underwater are magnified and appear nearer than they actually are. This distortion amounts to one-third, and a grasping hand often clutches futilely at a rope which is still inches away. Experience underwater soon corrects this error as far as the diver is concerned, and he will focus the camera at the correct distance. But the camera never learns to correct the error and so produces pictures out of focus.

It is all very difficult, and the author would suggest, without any claim to being an expert photographer, that the best solution is to use a lens that can make the best use of the light available, and by using a fast film, 'stop' down as much as possible and thereby achieve a maximum depth of focus, which will tolerate a lot of error.

VISIBILITY

Although the visibility in west channel and west coast waters can be excellent for sport and exploration, it leaves something to be desired from the photographer's point of view. Sand in suspension causes most of the underwater fog. This sand is stirred up from the bottom by tidal currents, and is added to by the mud and sand brought down the rivers after heavy rain. The water visibility is several times better during the period of neap tides and during quiet weather, and this should be borne in mind when planning underwater expeditions. Plankton fog will also reduce visibility and is at its worst during the spring. This sand in suspension, and plankton, causes the natural blue sea to become green. The colour of the sea is a direct indication of its transparency, and the deeper the blue the clearer the water will be. The deepest blue seas are found in the North Atlantic, the Sargasso Sea, the tropical Pacific and the Indian Ocean. Arctic seas are green and our own North Sea is the greenest of all. A really distinct demarcation line exists between the really blue water of the Atlantic and the greeny-blue seas of home waters, in the latitude of Ushant, perhaps a hundred miles off-shore. It is quite remarkable. One moment the boat is gliding across deep blue space, with every appearance of being unsupported, like an airship against the blue sky—and then the next time you look—just a boat floating in sea-water, with England right ahead.

The greatest recorded transparency is that of the Sargasso Sea, where a white disc, 6 ft in diameter, could still be seen from the

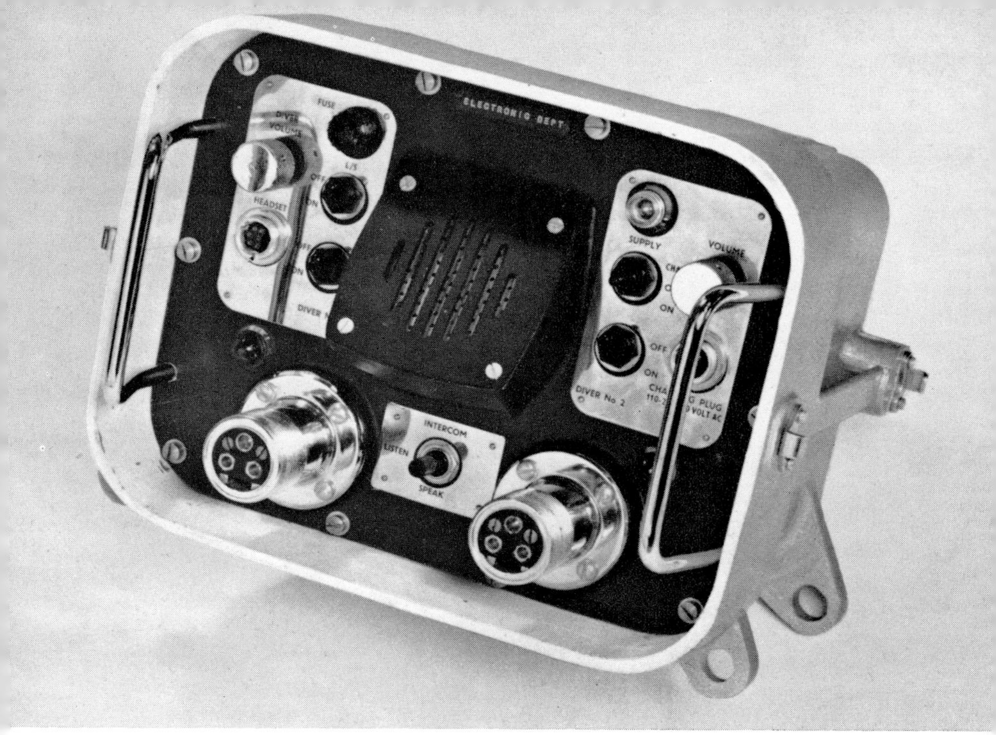

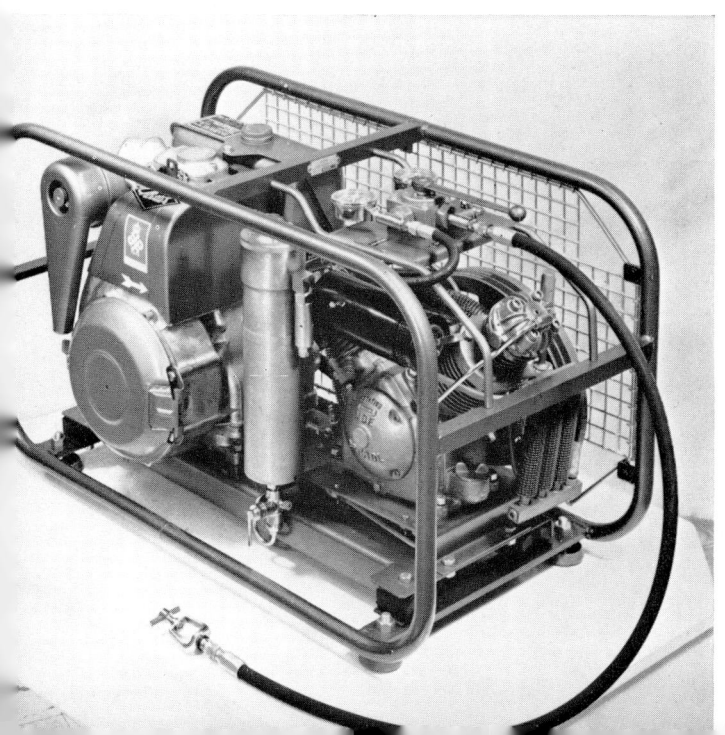

Page 125 (*above*) Standard diver telephone for two divers; (*below*) portable compressor unit for the filling of aqualung cylinders

Page 126 (*above*) Submersible decompression chamber; (*below*) submersible decompression and recompression chamber

surface at a depth of 216 ft. During calm weather, well out in the west channel, the same disc might be seen at 150 ft, and in the North Sea it disappears at around 60 ft during the quietest weather, and at only 30 ft in rough weather.

Tests have also been concluded to determine how deep the sunlight can penetrate. In the Mediterranean a photographic plate turned dark at 1,200-ft depth, but in mid-Atlantic the same experiment darkened the plate at nearly 5,000 ft. The light value in shallow water is higher than one would expect, especially on a light sandy bottom, but even so, an exposure of at least four times that required on the surface will be required.

Water acts as a colour filter and removes the longer wave lengths at the red end of the visible spectrum first. It is undoubtedly the shorter more penetrating wave lengths, probably outside the range of the visible spectrum, that discoloured the photographic plate at such great depths. As light travels through water, more and more of the longer wave lengths at the red end of the spectrum are filtered out, leaving only the more penetrating shorter wave lengths from the blue end of the spectrum beyond 30 ft. Colour photography beyond these depths is therefore a waste of time, unless artificial light is available. Again, at a distance beyond 30 ft the long wave lengths from the artificial light are absorbed, leaving the distant background deep blue or purple.

Many of the grotto-like chasms explored off the Devon coast, in 70 ft of water, impressive as they are with their giant sea-anemones and powdering of starfish, would take on added beauty nearer the surface. The beauty of these depths is that of utter peace. A fish hangs motionless in the near distance, before gliding off with an imperceptible movement of the tail to pastures new. An edible crab as large as a tea tray clings to a vertical wall of rock, and only floats down in slow motion, when disturbed, blending into the stony ground as you watch. The anemones and starfish remain a decoration in this motionless, silent world.

The diver, the first living man since time began, trespassing in this world of grey and blue, is struck with awe by the very unearthliness of the prehistoric world before him. His dancing silver bubbles, expanding as they rise, trace the shortest path through time, bubbling into life amongst the primitive starfish of three hundred million years ago, and ending in the wind-blown world of today. On the prompting of an internal tremor, our explorer ascends effortlessly up his stairway of time, every bubble representing a million years, to drag himself forth, a slave of gravitation in the chosen world of man.

12
UNDERWATER WORK

HAVING mastered the technique of diving, and become proficient in the use of the various types of breathing apparatus, a man or woman can in no way be guaranteed a living. Unfortunately, no one is prepared to pay a man to dive, but only for the work done underwater. If a man shows little practical initiative out of the water, he will be more than useless on the bottom, and if he is too superior for manual labouring in his own element, the romance of 'underwater work' will soon begin to fade.

The navy has trained men of different trades to use underwater breathing apparatus so they can get to the working site for their particular job. The organisation is a large one with everything laid on, and as far as the diver is concerned, time and money do not count. The free-lance civilian diver has to be a 'jack-of-all-trades', with more than his share of common sense, together with ingrained seamanship. He will be asked to accomplish the impossible at times, not from spite, but from faith. He is usually called in when everything else has failed, and for brief moments becomes the hinge pin on which the whole job hangs. Tough engineers will pander to his smallest request, but they must be reasonable, and the diver must not take advantage of the situation.

In the past the diver has not commanded a high place in the social scale, but there is a new outlook today and people from all walks of life are venturing into the depths—civil engineers, marine surveyors, marine artists, together with marine biologists and archaeologists are among the pupils training as free-divers and/or standard divers.

Apart from underwater surveys, search, and recovery, most methods of constructional and demolition work can be carried out efficiently by the diver, sometimes more easily than on dry land. Concrete will set better underwater than in the atmosphere. If mixed with grouting fluid, according to the maker's instructions, underwater concreting is much simplified. The large stones which form the aggregate can be dumped underwater first, and the grout is then poured down a pipe extending from the surface, into the aggregate, under the control of the diver. The grouting mixture will not readily mix with water, so very little is lost.

A common practise is to mix up dry concrete mixture, and put up in sandbags. These are laid in courses by the diver, the water percolates into the mixture through the sacking. The necessary chemical action takes place, and good hard concrete results. The sandbag material soon rots away. When labour costs outweigh the extra cost of the pure cement, it is often practical to lay the pure cement as supplied in the stiff brown paper bags. After two days underwater they are quite hard, and during the course of time become as hard as stone.

Metal and wood may be sawn underwater as on land, but in the case of wood, especially soft wood, a little extra set on the teeth of the saw is an advantage. Also the use of augers for drilling holes in wooden piles, etc, and hand-drills is quite normal practice. The threading of metal bolts and studs, and threading of internal holes, can be accomplished in the normal way with taps and dies.

A spade can be called anything but a spade underwater, but a pickaxe is just as efficient a tool as on dry land. For large operations, most of the above tools can be supplied powered by compressed air. Pneumatic tools for use underwater are modified by having the air outlet exhausting through a second rubber hose at the surface.

If a series of piles are to be cut through it is easier to drill a row of holes nearly touching each other, before cutting through with a wood saw. To facilitate the drilling of the holes, a template is made of hardwood or metal, which is then clamped to the pile. In the case of individual unsupported piles, it will be necessary to apply a steady strain at the top, in order to keep the saw cut open. It is usually required to cut piles at a level below that of the sea or river bed, as a row of submerged stumps will be a nuisance or even a danger to shipping. A high pressure water hose is ideal for this sort of work. Using a portable pump similar to the model used by the fire services, the author finds that a pressure of 50 psi being ejected through a $\tfrac{3}{4}$-in diameter nozzle is most effective. Providing the diver has something to hold, he can just manage this pressure, and holes 3 or 4 ft deep can be blown in sand and gravel in a matter of minutes. A line secured to the nozzle and passed round the pile or other object and held by the diver, will relieve him of a lot of strain.

With such a powerful jet reaction, the large brass nozzle can be a menace if allowed to run amok. Special nozzles designed to expend some of its energy at 180 degrees to the main outlet nozzle, will make the work much easier for the diver. A much higher pressure can then be used, which will compensate for splitting the effective stream.

Very often a sunken vessel will settle so deeply into soft mud that a hose is required to tunnel underneath before the hull can be slung ready for lifting. However, in most cases, with vessels up to 100 tons, a wire passed through the propeller aperture and another well under the forefoot will suffice. The four ends are then hove taut at low water, and belayed on board a suitable vessel, or pontoon, lying over the wreck. The rising tide is then used to lift the wreck off the bottom, and it is then moved inshore until it grounds. The operation is repeated until the falling tide leaves the hull high and dry, or sufficiently out of the water for pumps to be got working, the diver having already sealed off any water inlets or damage. In tideless waters, camels can be sunk in suitable positions and secured to the hull by divers. Air is then pumped into the camels to obtain the positive buoyancy required. Do not, for the moment, imagine that raising sunken vessels is accomplished without other complications, but they can usually be solved by good seamanship and common sense as the job progresses.

Marine archaeologists are loath to use pressure jets in uncovering priceless historic wrecks, as they picture the surface effect of a fireman's hose. In actual fact, when used underwater, the efflux can barely be felt 3 or 4 ft from the nozzle. Used in conjunction with a suction pump, it can be a most useful underwater tool.

Another very useful underwater tool is the Cox Submarine Bolt Driving and Punching Gun. It is explosively-actuated by a black powder charge incorporated in the bolt or punching ammunition. The barrels are loaded out of the water, but the diver can remain submerged with the gun, having spare loaded barrels sent down to him. It will drive solid bolts of $\frac{5}{8}$ in diameter or hollow air bolts of $\frac{3}{4}$ in diameter through steel plate up to 1 in thick. The hollow air bolts have a detachable pointed nose, which can be unscrewed from the outside by inserting a screwdriver through the bolt. An adaptor can then be screwed on which will take a standard diver's air pipe, or a $\frac{3}{4}$-in BSP hose connection. Air can then be fed in for lifting or breathing purposes.

Holes can be punched of 11/16 in diameter in $\frac{3}{4}$-in thick steel plate, suitable for the bolt ammunition. For the timber patching of damaged steel hulls, extension bolts are supplied. The steel bolts are first fired through the existing hole in the timber into the steel hull, and then the extension bolts are screwed on to them. This method ensures that the bolts are lined up with the holes in the timber. A wooden ferrule is threaded over the extention bolt, which fits tightly into the hole in the timber. A washer and wing nut are then run down and tightened, securing the timber to the hull. Other applications of the Cox gun include the construction of cofferdams, and the punching out of loose rivets in ships' hulls, which are then plugged with wooden rivet plugs.

Smaller and simpler bolt firing guns are also available, which make use of a $\frac{3}{8}$-in waterproof cartridge. They will fire steel bolts that leave a $\frac{3}{8}$-in threaded stud projecting, on to which $\frac{1}{2}$-in threaded adaptors can then be screwed, being a more practical size for securing timber patches. Headed steel nails are also supplied, for pinning steel patches directly on to a steel, concrete or timber base.

13

UNDERWATER CUTTING AND WELDING

GAS CUTTING

UNDOUBTEDLY, one of the most valuable tools available to the diver is the oxy-hydrogen underwater cutting apparatus. The principle on which both surface and underwater gas cutting equipment works is that of heating a ferrous metal to a suitable temperature, and then directing a jet of pure oxygen on to the preheated area. The metal is rapidly oxidised in the path of the oxygen stream, and a 'kerf' or cut is obtained. By moving the torch slowly and steadily across the metal a continuous line of cut is maintained.

Before attempting to use an underwater cutter the diver should obtain experience with oxy-acetylene surface cutting apparatus. Oxy-acetylene apparatus can be used a few feet underwater, but as acetylene is not safe when used at pressures exceeding 30 psi hydrogen is used with a specially designed underwater torch. Underwater cutting can then be carried out at all practical depths. The underwater cutting torch has an additional air supply, which is directed by an outer cowl to form a pocket of air in the water in which the cutting flame can work.

When assembling the apparatus, blow a little gas through pipes and fittings to clear them of any foreign matter. No oil must be used to lubricate the apparatus, owing to the presence of oxygen. Connect up the battery (which is required so that the torch can be lit underwater, to the striking plate, making the plate negative and the torch positive. Open up the gas supply on one of each of the three pairs of cylinders, keeping the other cylinders in reserve. Set the gas pressures on the master gauges for the depth of water and thickness of metal to be cut according to the tables, with the valves of the cutter fully open.

When setting the oxygen pressure, the cutting oxygen valve must be open, as well as the oxygen screw down valve. Having set the pressures and tested the torch on the surface, using valves on cutter for the surface test, close cutter valves and extinguish flame. The striking plate should be secured to the torch by several feet of light line, so that the diver can find it easily. The torch is then lowered to the diver by way of the shot rope, or a specially set up leading wire, with the air valve open. This prevents water from entering the torch. The diver clears the line of cut with a scraper and wire brush before lighting the torch.

A simple method of passing tools, etc down to the diver, is to secure them with a short piece of line to the breast rope. The diver then hauls down until the tool arrives, removes, it, and then signals for the slack breast rope to be taken up again.

When ready, the diver signals to the surface for the battery current to be switched on. The hydrogen valve is opened half a turn. Always operate hydrogen valve first. Then the oxygen valve is opened. Rub cutter across striking plate, and the torch will ignite with a dull explosion, followed by a continuous roar. The diver signals for the battery current to be switched off, and he is now ready to commence.

If a backfire occurs, shut the hydrogen valve. Open it again, and if combustion has ceased, relight in normal way. If persistent backfiring occurs, check surface pressures. Low air pressure may be the trouble. An excess of oxygen will also promote backfiring, or an excess of hydrogen will help to overcome the trouble, but also tends to increase preheating time. A worn or enlarged jet annulus will cause backfiring.

To commence cutting, when using a serrated hooded cutter, place flame squarely on edge of work, but with a plain hooded cutter, tilt torch so that gases can escape freely. Preheat the metal to an orange glow, about five seconds, then operate oxygen cutting stream lever. Draw cutter slowly and smoothly along line of cut. If the cutting action ceases, through moving too fast or for any other reason, the oxygen cutting stream must be turned off and the metal preheated at the point where the cut

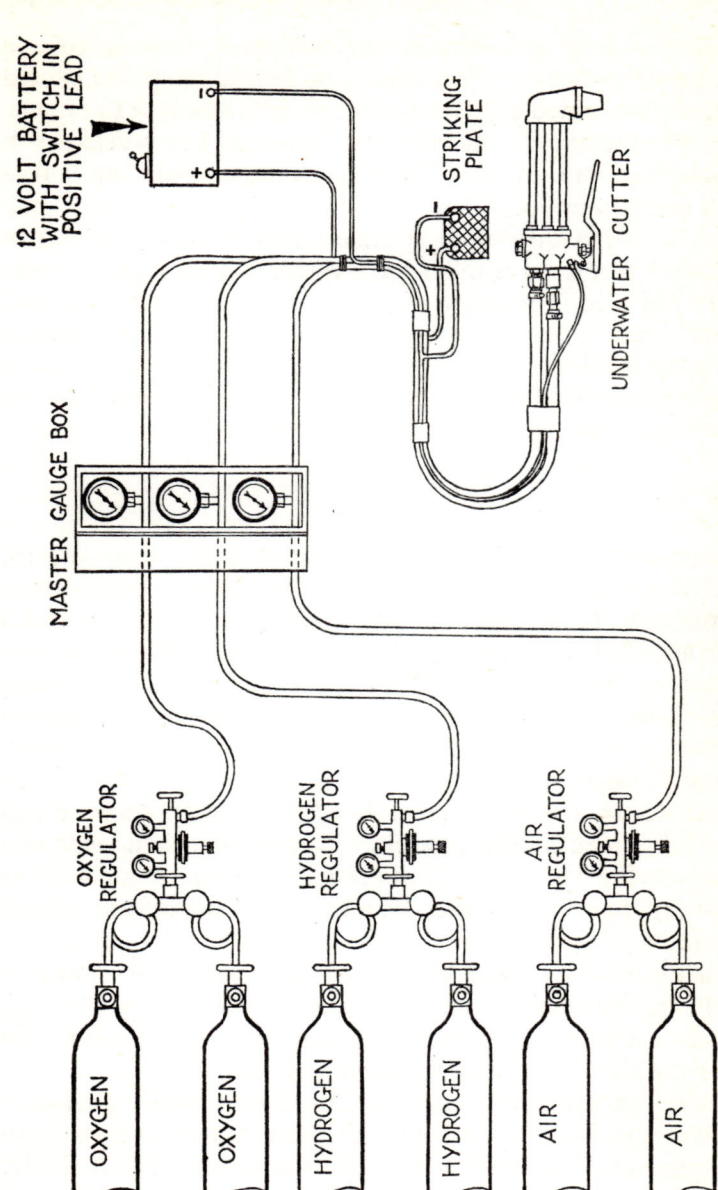

Underwater cutting apparatus

was lost. If a cut has to be commenced away from an edge, a hole must be pierced. The cutter is held steady over the chosen spot, and preheated until the flame changes from blue to orange, then open the oxygen cutting valve. A hole of $\frac{1}{8}$ in diameter will be obtained, and this is enlarged by continuing the cut with a small rotary motion.

The oxygen-hydrogen torch will cut iron or steel, but if any of the yellow metals have to be cut, oxy-arc-cutting apparatus will have to be used. This apparatus will also cut iron and steel, but the maximum depth of cut is 2 in, and if a clean cut is required, $\frac{1}{2}$ in is the maximum. However, a second cut can be taken, so it is possible to plough through thicker material, limited only by the every increasing length of the electrode.

OXY-ARC CUTTING

The oxy-arc underwater torch is a simple piece of apparatus, consisting of an electrode holder, with the oxygen cutting stream fed through the hollow electrode. Carbon and steel electrodes are available, but the former are generally used in Britain as they last longer. A trigger valve is incorporated in the torch handle, which controls the oxygen cutting stream. One firm manufactures an oxy-arc underwater cutting torch which has no manually operated oxygen valve, the oxygen cutting stream being operated automatically. The valve is connected to the electrical circuit so that when an arc is struck, the circuit is completed and a solenoid ram opens the oxygen valve, allowing the cutting stream to flow. When the arc is broken, the solenoid cuts off the oxygen cutting stream.

The diver wears rubber gloves, and a coloured glass must be fitted over the helmet window. A supply of coated electrodes is carried by the diver. The work is usually made negative and the cutter positive, but it can be used either way.

The electrode holder is connected by a heavy cable to a generator on the surface. It must be a DC generator with a 500/600-amp capacity. The amperage required is between 325 and 375. The oxygen pressure is set on the surface reducing valve. The pressure required is 55 psi plus the pressure of the water at the working depth. This increases 1 psi for every 2·3 ft of depth,

Underwater Cutting and Welding

although it is usually near enough to treat it as a $\frac{1}{2}$ psi per foot of depth. An anti-flash valve will absorb another 5 psi.

Turn on the oxygen supply before lowering the torch to the diver so that water and any oil are excluded. Electrodes must be screwed home firmly by the diver, otherwise arcing may occur in the cutter.

The line of cut should first of all be scraped clean. To commence the cut, the end of the electrode has to be rubbed firmly on to the work to remove the protective coating. Arcing then takes place, the oxygen valve is triggered, and the cut made by following through slowly and steadily. When cutting non-ferrous materials, the speed of cut is reduced as they do not readily oxidise, and the process is that of melting the metal and blowing it away.

ARC WELDING

Underwater arc welding is a practical proposition for a diver well experienced in the technique. The current required is again DC, the amperage being between 175 and 185.

The work is made negative and the welding rod positive for downward and vertical welding, but with overhead welding, the connections are reversed. This is because the current is flowing from the negative lead and therefore assists in transferring the welding rod metal up to the position in which it is required.

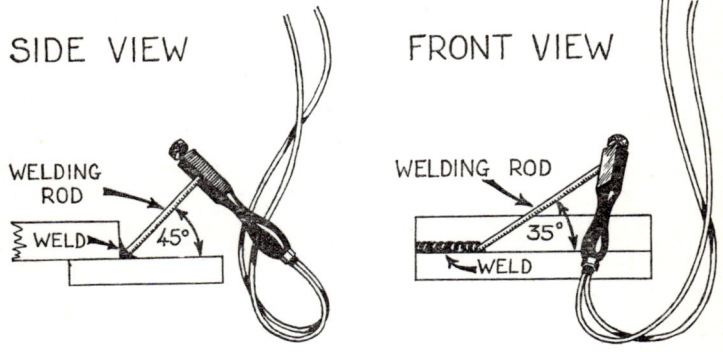

Arc welding torch

The end of the welding rod can be steadied by light pressure of one hand, the tip of the rod resting lightly on the plate to be welded. The welding rod should never be dragged along but allowed to work itself along against the push of the deposited metal. The rod should be held at the angles shown in the sketch below.

Before continuing a weld, always clear the slag from the previous weld with a stiff wire brush. Rubber gloves and the coloured glass are, of course, used as with oxy-arc cutting.

The normal welding rods used are No 6 and No 8, and the plate welded will not be more than $\frac{1}{2}$ in thick. Due to the brittleness of the weld, the welding of thicker plate is not recommended. All electrical connections must be clean and tight.

14

UNDERWATER BLASTING

THE use of explosives underwater often saves much energy and time. Their use by small operators does not involve a large capital outlay, and whilst practical instruction is desirable, it is not absolutely essential.

EXPLOSIVES AND FUSES

The most powerful explosive available is submarine blasting gelatine, and as it has a very high degree of water resistance, it is most suitable for use underwater. Blackpowder, or gunpowder, explosives are of no use underwater, owing to their low speed of burning, about 300 ft per second, which compares badly with the gelignites that have detonating velocities between 3,000 metres per second and 7,000 metres per second (10,000 to 23,000 ft per second), and the fact that they will not burn when damp.

Explosives for underwater blasting should have a high bulk strength, good water resistance, and should also be capable of retaining their sensitivity when subjected to hydrostatic pressure. A number of gelatinous explosives fulfil these requirements to a varying degree.

When explosives containing ammonium nitrate or sodium nitrate are submerged, the water gradually seeps into the explosive, the rate of penetration being dependent on the water pressure.

When the explosive is to be used immediately in under 20 ft of water, some of the lesser waterproof ammon-gelignites or straight gelignites (eg Polar-ammon-gelignite or Gelignite 62 per cent NG) may be used. Submarine blasting gelatine does not contain any hygroscopic salts and there is no possibility of water penetration or absorption.

Nobel-Glasgow Explosives recommended for Underwater Use

Explosive	Cartridge diameter (in)	Max depth of water (ft)	Max duration of immersion
Polar-ammon-gelatine dynamite	$\frac{7}{8}$–3 3–8	20 100	24 hours 7–30 days
Polar-ammon-gelignite	$\frac{7}{8}$–3 3–8	20 100	24 hours 7–30 days
Geophex	All sizes	1,200	72 hours
Submarine blasting gelatine	All sizes	1,200	Several weeks

Geophex can be supplied in Seislok coupling cartridges. These are used to assemble the explosives charge in a long rigid column of great convenience in charging underwater shot holes. Ammon Gelatines contain a proportion of water-soluble salts. When these explosives are immersed in water, the water gradually seeps into the cartridge at a rate dependent on the pressure. Thus the diameter of the dry core of the explosives is gradually reduced. The cartridge diameter should therefore be kept as large as possible.

Explosives susceptible to moisture can be used underwater, if the charge is made up in a waterproof container, such as a car inner tube. The entry of the detonating fuse or leading wires into the inner tube must be watertight.

DETONATORS

One method of exploding a charge is by using a safety fuse, and for underwater work, smokeless waterproof fuse is available. As it burns at a rate of 2 ft per minute, when working in a depth of more than 10 ft, it is time saving to include a length of

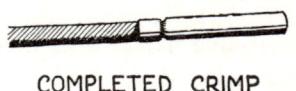

COMPLETED CRIMP

USING CRIMPERS TO ATTACH
DETONATOR TO SAFETY FUSE

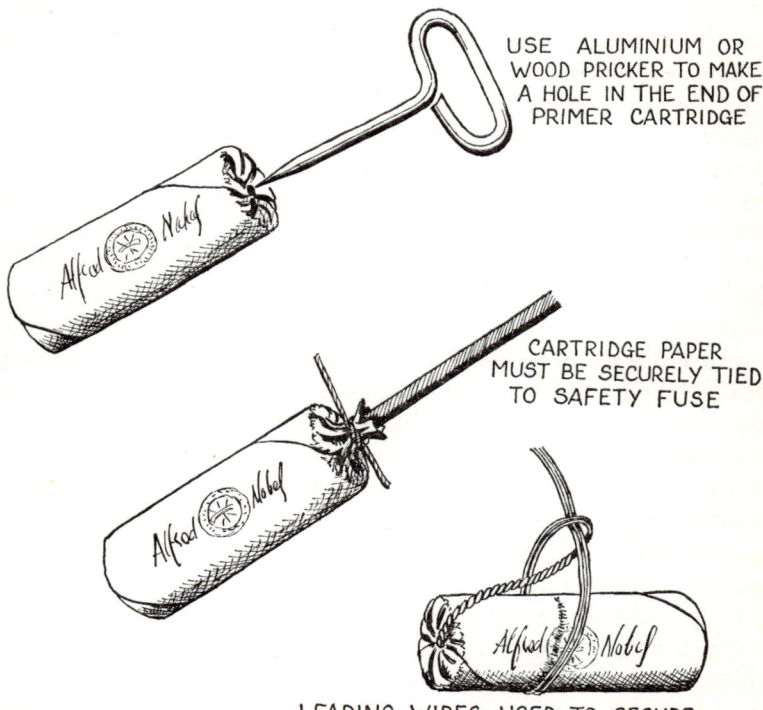

USE ALUMINIUM OR
WOOD PRICKER TO MAKE
A HOLE IN THE END OF
PRIMER CARTRIDGE

CARTRIDGE PAPER
MUST BE SECURELY TIED
TO SAFETY FUSE

LEADING WIRES USED TO SECURE
ELECTRIC DETONATOR TO PRIMER CARTRIDGE

Attaching detonator and safety fuse to cartridge

Cordtex in the fuse line. Cordtex is a detonating instantaneous fuse.

An explosive charge is made up of cartridges, one of which has a detonator inserted. We call this cartridge the primer. The detonator has a length of safety fuse inserted into one end, which initiates the detonator, and in turn initiates the primer cartridge which, being in contact with the other cartridges, fires off the whole charge.

It is convenient to use capped fuses. These fuses are supplied in suitable lengths with the detonator already crimped on efficiently. This ensures a waterproof joint and reduces the chance of a misfire. However, it is more usual to make up the fuse line. Cut the fuse straight across with a clean, sharp knife or fuse-cutter, using a freshly cut end for insertion into the detonator. Never allow the ends to come into contact with damp, oil or grease. Slip the detonator over the end of the fuse, so that the composition and fuse are in contact. Hold the fuse lightly pressed against the composition, but do not screw in; crimp the detonator gently but securely on to the fuse with approved crimpers.

For underwater work, insulation tape must be used to waterproof the joint between the detonator and the safety fuse. From experience at the British Underwater Centre, it has been noted that the speed of burning of safety fuse underwater, is slightly increased. Normally, it is better to secure the safety fuse to a float, so that it cannot sink down after lighting. If there is a misfire, the safety fuse and detonator can then be recovered and a second length of fuse and detonator can be secured to the Cordtex, which is always used except in very shallow water.

Open a cartridge of explosive, make a hole with an aluminium brass or wood pricker in the opened out end and push in the detonator, leaving the top of it projecting. Tie the paper cartridge firmly round the fuse immediately above the detonator.

If including a length of Cordtex, the Cordtex is used as the detonator to fire the primer cartridge, and the Cordtex is initiated by a No 6 or No 8 plain or electric detonator. The detonators must point along the Cordtex fuse towards the explosive charge, and must be firmly secured with adhesive tape or string so that the bottom of the detonator is in close contact

Page 143 (*above*) Capillary type depth gauge; (*below*) 150-watt sealed beam underwater lamp

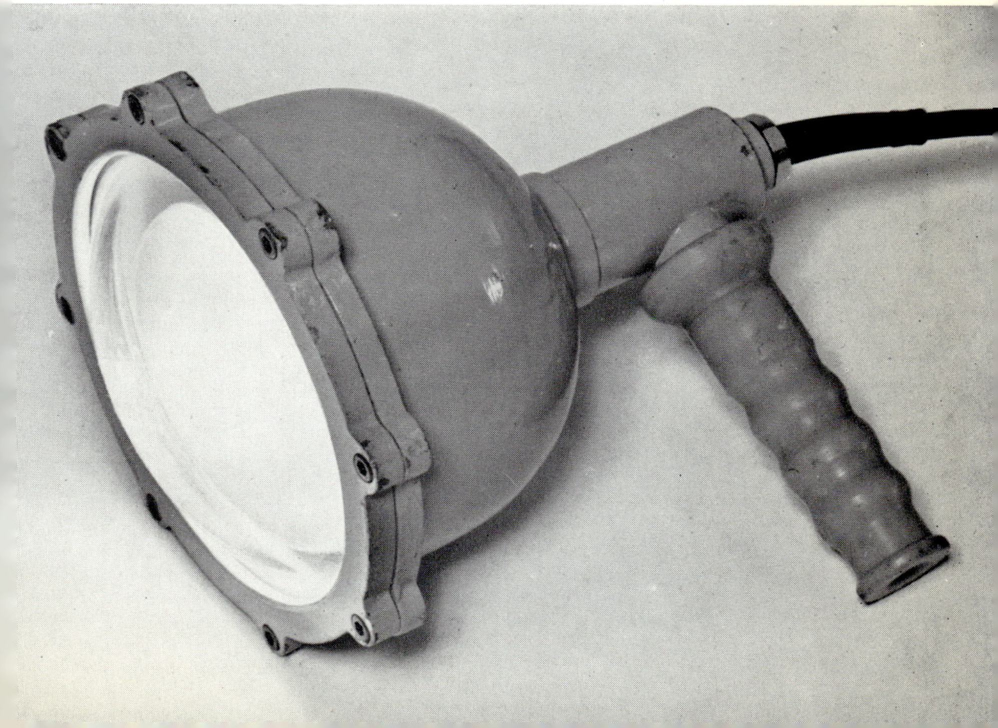

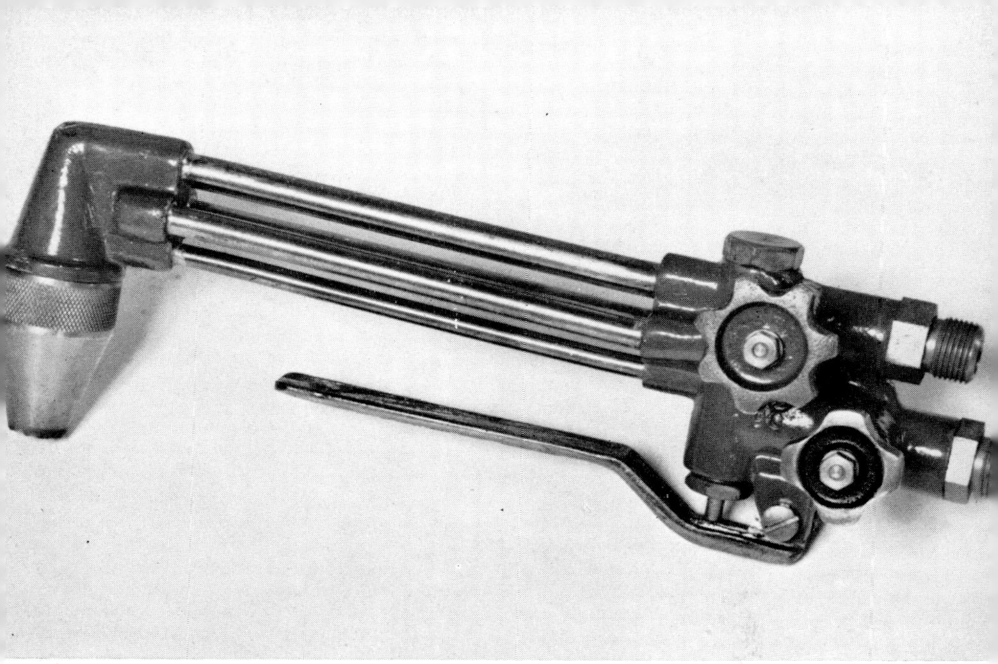

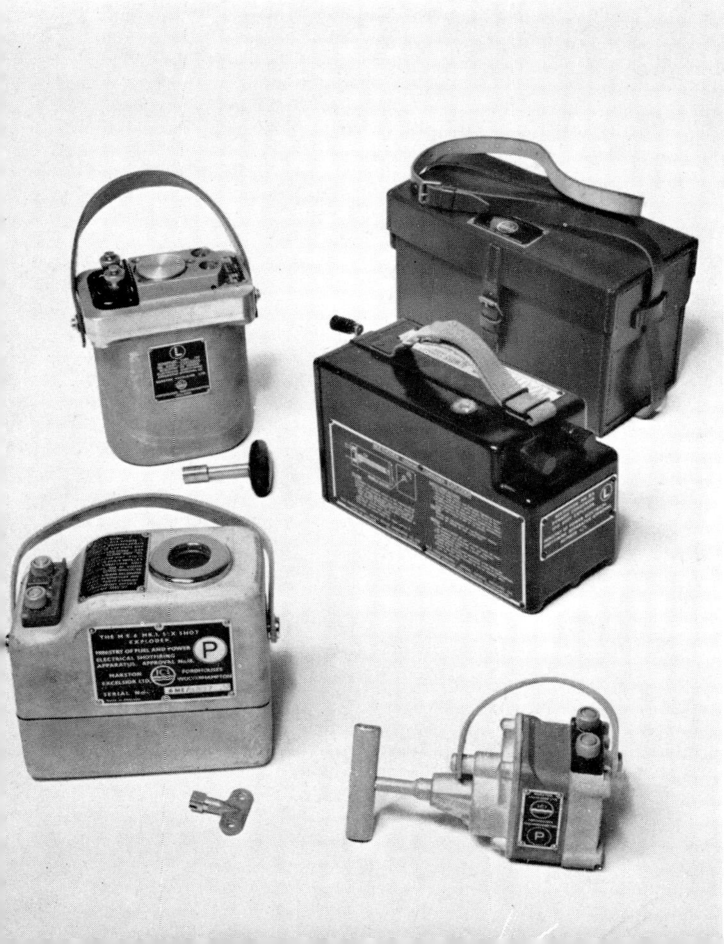

Page 144 (*above*) Vixen oxy-hydrogen underwater cutting torch; (*below*) various types of exploders

Underwater Blasting

with the side of the detonating fuse. Cordtex is a fuse with a high explosive core as distinct from the blackpowder core in safety fuse. It detonates at a rate of 7,000 metres per second.

To ensure satisfactory initiation of the primer, an adequate length of Cordtex fuse must be in contact with the primer cartridge, and it should be fixed so that it cannot readily be pulled out of the cartridge.

Where more than one explosive charge is being initiated, it is necessary to join branch lines from each charge to the main line to which the detonator is attached. It is most important to consider the direction in which the detonation wave will be travelling at the junction, since failures may arise if the branch line is not attached in the right way. Where the main line is a straight length of Cordtex initiated from one end, the 'L' joint may be used, but care must be taken to see that the branch line leads off in the same direction as the detonation wave to ensure propagation of the branch line.

Another joint is the clove hitch; with this no allowance need be made for the direction of the wave, as the branch line will pick up from whichever side the detonation wave arrives. Where the main line is initiated simultaneously at both ends, as in a ring main, the detonation wave may arrive at the branch junction from either side and a double 'L' joint or the clove hitch joint must be used. The clove hitch joint is usually quicker and simpler to make, but care should be taken to see that the knot is tight. Whichever joint is used, the branch line should be in close contact with the main line and should be secured with thin wire, or with string or adhesive tape. With the single or double 'L' joints there should be at least 2 in of the branch line in contact with the main.

Occasionally it will be necessary to join lengths of Cordtex fuse, and this can be done by binding the lengths side by side with adhesive tape, thin wire or string, making sure that the fuse is in good contact and will not readily pull apart. An overlap of about 3 in should be used.

Cordtex detonating fuse is invaluable for submarine blasting operations because of its waterproof quality. With a few additional precautions it can be used confidently in water up to 60 ft in depth. At such depths moisture cannot enter the fuse through

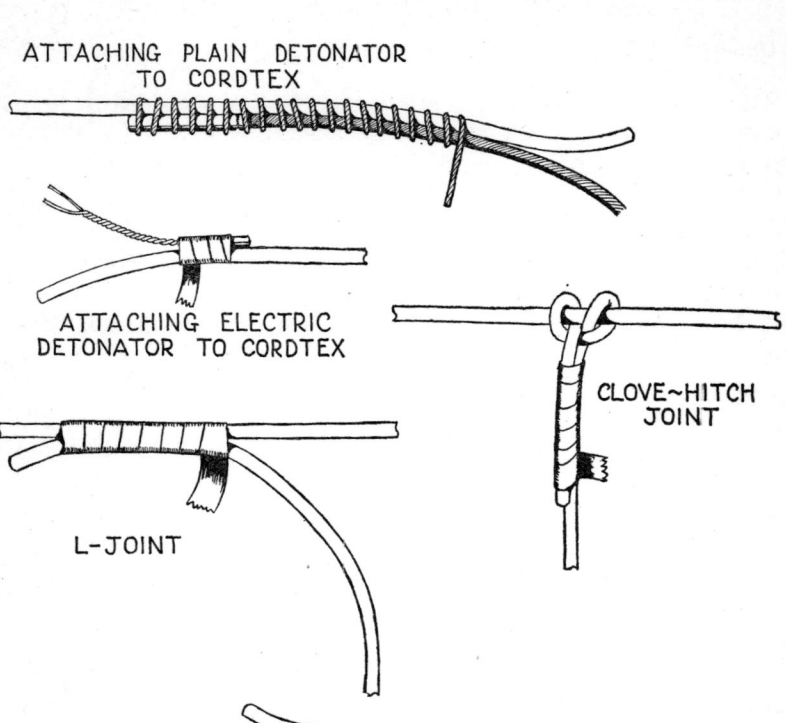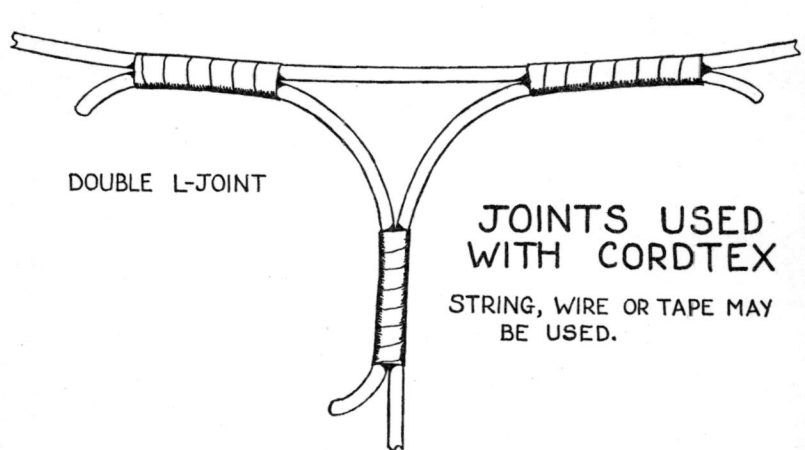

the plastic outer covering, but it may penetrate along the core from the cut end. Provided initiation is adequate the detonation wave will continue throughout a length of wet Cordtex fuse with full velocity and power.

If a length of Cordtex fuse so wetted is opposite the detonator or forms that part of a branch line in contact with the main line, propagation failures may occur because such a form of side blow may not detonate wet Cordtex fuse with certainty. The detonation wave will, however, pass from dry to wet fuse in the same length of Cordtex. The receptor Cordtex at a joint or opposite a detonator must be dry.

Under damp conditions or heads of 1 or 2 ft of water the rate of moisture creep along the core is about 1 ft in 24 hours, and the best method of ensuring the dry line is to leave an adequate free end. At greater depths or where some days may pass before a charge is fired, empty detonator tubes should be crimped on the ends of the Cordtex fuse and the crimped joint made waterproof with a sealing compound. Cordtex fuse with a wet core can be initiated by a commercial waterproof primer with a No 6 Thistle Brand detonator or by crimping a short dry piece of Cordtex fuse end to end with the wet line by means of a copper sleeve.

Except when single shots are to be fired, Cordtex detonating fuse is almost indispensable for successful underwater blasting. It is easily handled by divers and is sufficiently robust to withstand the strains experienced. Cordtex can be used as an explosive charge by itself. It possesses a high velocity of detonation (7,000 metres per second). Cast iron pipes and plates can be cut by winding Cordtex round them. A 10 in diameter pipe, 9/16 in thick can be cleanly cut by winding five turns of Cordtex round the circumference, two turns being placed on top of three. Small wooden piles can be similarly cut providing enough Cordtex is used. Again, several strands of Cordtex can be used in shot holes instead of the usual cartridge. It is supplied in 500-ft reels with an explosive weight of $3\frac{1}{2}$ lb.

ELECTRIC FIRING

An alternative method of firing explosive charges is by using an electric current to initiate an electric detonator, which is used with a primer cartridge, in the same way as with a safety fuse. A modern commercial electric detonator consists of a thin-walled tube of either aluminium or copper, closed at one end, which contains a base charge, a priming charge and a fuse-head. The open end of the tube is sealed with a neoprene plug through which the leading wires of the fuse-head assembly pass.

The electric fuse-head consists of two metal foils separated by a layer of insulation. The leading wires are soldered to the base of the foils, and a very fine wire connects their tips. Round this wire a bead of igniting composition is formed which is usually built up of several layers, the innermost layer being readily ignited by heat. The resistance of the fuse-head alone, without leading wires, is usually kept between the limits of 0·9 and 1·6 ohms, and a current of 0·5 amp applied for 50 milliseconds will fire it, although under field conditions an appreciably greater current should be supplied.

When an electric fuse assembly is crimped in a charged detonator tube, the ordinary electric detonator is formed. Every stage of manufacture of the electric fuse-head assembly is care-

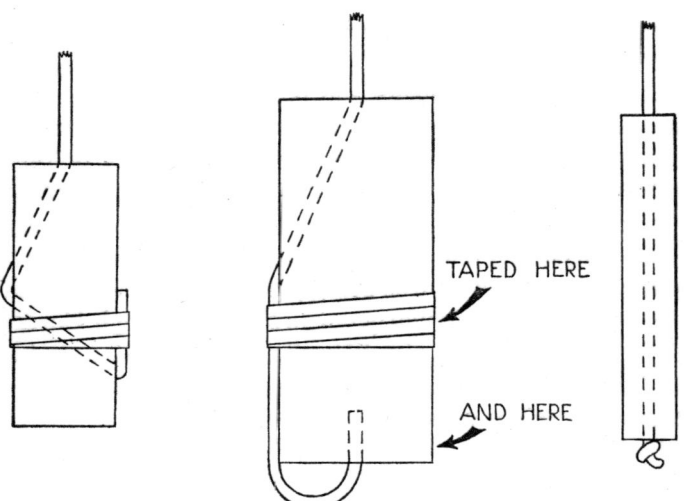

Methods of preparing the primer cartridge with Cordtex

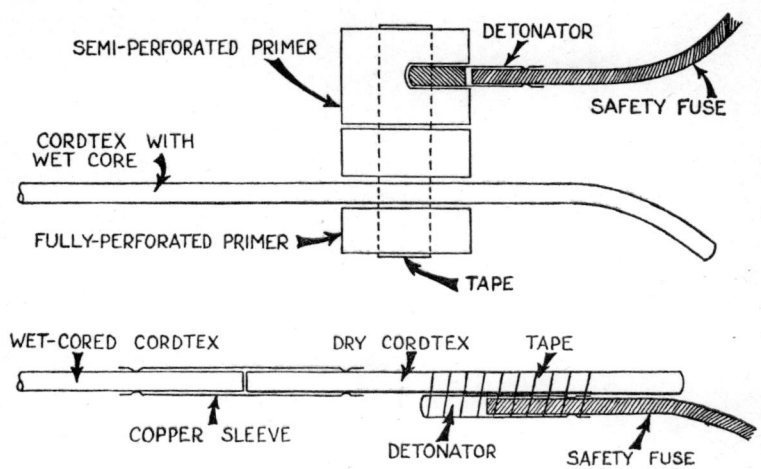

Initiation of wet Cordtex

fully controlled, as also is the manufacture of the detonator itself, so that the characteristics and performance are consistent and reliable. ICI manufacture electric detonators for underwater use (waterproof and submarine types). Waterproof electric detonators are fitted with plastic-covered leading wires and will withstand a water pressure of 30 lb psi. Submarine electric detonators are designed to function under high hydrostatic pressures and will fire satisfactorily under pressures of 60 psi.

Nobel-Glasgow submarine electric detonators are specially manufactured to prevent water under high pressures from reaching the detonator composition. They are fitted with plastic-covered tinned copper leading wires and are tested to withstand a water pressure of 60 psi (equivalent to a head of 138 ft of water) for at least 16 hours, and they will normally function at much greater depths and for longer periods of immersion. They have, in fact, been used satisfactorily under pressures corresponding to 1,200 ft of water. Nobel-Glasgow delay detonators and short-delay detonators will withstand similar water pressures. To obtain the maximum effect with Geophex or submarine blasting gelatine the detonators used must be of the aluminium tube type and, if possible, star strength.

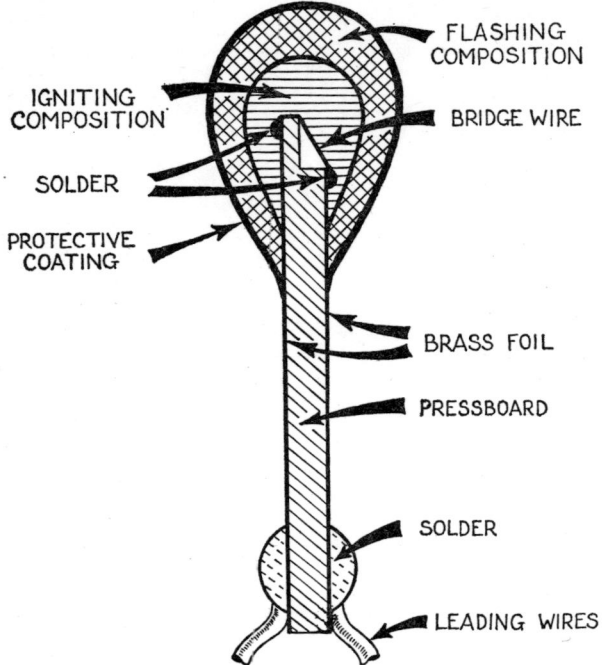

Electric fuse-head:

DELAY DETONATORS

For certain blasting operations it is an advantage to have the various charges fired in predetermined sequence, with regular time intervals between the shots. This will reduce the maximum detonation wave when working close to structures that may suffer from water borne shock and ground vibration.

In all underwater blasting, consideration must be given to the possibility of water-borne shock waves causing damage to adjacent shipping or structures. With unconfined charges a high percentage of the energy goes to producing shock waves, and a charge of 50 lb will produce a perceptible effect on ships 200 yd away. When explosive charges are placed in boreholes the waterborne shock wave is not great. For instance, experience has shown that the waterborne shock wave was not perceptible

Underwater Blasting

in ships 200 yd from the blast when a 1,800 lb total weight of explosive divided into six 300-lb charges in boreholes was fired with short-delay intervals by means of detonating relays.

A drawing of a delay detonator is shown below. It will be seen that the assembly is like that of a standard electric detonator, but that a special delay element has been introduced between the fusehead and the base charge. This delay element consists of a thick-walled metal tube loaded with a column of slow-burning composition. When the fuse-head fires, it ignites the upper surface of this column, and the composition then burns slowly and uniformly downwards until it reaches the other end of the column and ignites the initiating explosive.

Two types of delay detonators are made, the half-second delay series and the short-delay series. The short-delay series is of particular importance where ground vibration must be kept to a minimum. Half-second delays and short-delays can be distinguished by the insulation of the leading wires, the half-second

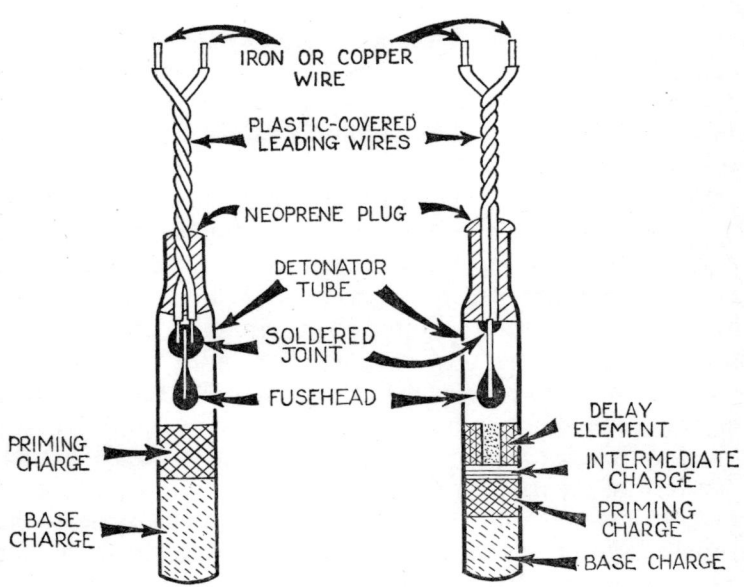

(*left*) standard electric detonator;
(*right*) delay detonator

series having one red and one yellow wire, and the short-delay series two red wires. Both series of delay detonators will withstand a water pressure of 60 psi.

Delay detonators can be coupled in series or parallel in the same way as ordinary electric detonators. The fuse-heads of all detonators ignite as the firing current passes, but the actual detonations occur only after the respective delay elements have burnt through. Accordingly, the breaking of the electrical circuit by the earlier delays has no effect on the firing of the latter ones.

EXPLODERS

An exploder is necessary to supply the low tension current required by the electric detonator. They are supplied with firing capacities suitable for single shot, six shot, thirty shot and one hundred shot firing. An example is the Little Demon, which is a single-shot exploder of the magneto type, housed in a robust cast aluminium casing. It is operated by a half-turn of the detachable firing key.

To test a single-shot exploder, one low-tension electric detonator should be fired in series with a non-inductive resistance of not less than 15 ohms, having a current-carrying capacity of over 0·5 amp. Three positive results in succession indicate that the instrument is satisfactory.

Multi-shot exploders may be tested by firing two detonators connected in series through a non-inductive resistance of such a value that the total resistance of the testing circuit is equal to that of the number of detonators the exploder is rated to fire. The two detonators are required in the circuit to show that the current is built up without time-lag. They must be covered to protect the operator against flying fragments. For these exploder tests the required non-inductive resistance can be supplied in the form of a rheostat, but any suitable resistance box may be used.

To test an electric detonator, it is placed in an iron tube or pipe as a safety measure. Its leading wires are then applied to the terminals of a circuit tester. If the needle moves, the detonator is fit for use; no movement shows that it is faulty.

To test a cable for continuity, join the two leads at one end and apply the other ends to the terminals of a circuit tester. A

Underwater Blasting

movement of the needle indicates continuity; no deflection shows there is a break in one or other of the leads.

To test for a short circuit, separate the two leads at one end and apply the leads at the other end to a circuit tester. Any deflection of the needle indicates a short circuit which must be investigated and rectified; no deflection indicates that the cable is sound. ICI ohm-meters are usually set to zero resistance and on applying to such a circuit the needle would swing over to infinity. With direct reading ohm-meter, allow 2 ohms per detonator and add cable resistance.

Immediately before firing a round of shots, the whole circuit should be tested for continuity. If a fault is discovered, the following procedure should be adopted:

> Check cable and detonator connections.
> Disconnect the shot-firing cable and retest.
> If the cable is in order, test each detonator individually. To do this, the leads must be disconnected and each in turn attached to the ends of the cable. The tests should be made from the firing point—at a safe distance from the shothole.

All types of electric detonators may be used for single-shot firing. A hole is made with a wooden, brass or aluminium pricker in the end of the primer cartridge, and the detonator inserted until it is buried. The leading wires are then hitched round the cartridge to prevent the detonator from being withdrawn. The bared ends of the detonator leading wires should not be allowed to wave about, as sometimes an electric detonator can be fired by stray currents picked up from electric power units. In fact, it is as well to remove all sources of electric supply. Electric shot-firing should be stopped if an electrical storm is in progress. The bared ends of the leading wires are next cleaned and attached to the shot-firing cable.

Joint insulators are available in two sizes, B1—3·7 mm × 55 mm long and B2—5·7 mm × 78 mm long. These are aluminium tubes covered with white pvc and filled with petroleum jelly. The connections are made by twisting the wires tightly together and inserting the joint into the tube; the tube is then bent double to anchor the leads.

When the diver has placed the charge and left the water, then, and then only, should the other end of the cable be attached to the exploder at the firing station and the shot be fired.

Many shot firing operations involve the simultaneous firing of a number of charges, and the method normally employed is to fire a number of ordinary electric detonators connected with the exploder through the shot-firing cable in a simple series circuit.

When firing a number of shots electrically in series the actual procedure is the same as single-shot firing, but the lengths of leading wire extending from each charge are coiled down at the firing station until all the explosive charges are placed.

The person in charge of the operation should never allow the handle of the exploder to be out of his possession. He should never entrust the job of joining up the charge to anyone else. If the diver has to return to a charge, first disconnect the cable from the exploder and remove the handle. Never allow a firing cable to be dragged along, but see that it is coiled and carried carefully. Take every precaution to prevent kinking, as internal breaks are difficult to trace. All blasting appliances must be kept dry and in good working order.

A misfire should be treated with the greatest care. The regulations stipulate that no person shall be allowed near a charge unless it has exploded or until an interval has elapsed of not less than thirty minutes in the case of firing by fuse or ten minutes in the case of firing by electricity. If the charge is being fired electrically, the cable must be disconnected and the handle removed from the exploder. Any faults can then be remedied and the shot fired.

If a misfire cannot be accounted for, a second charge should be placed next to the misfired charge. After firing, a careful search should be made for undetonated explosives.

It will be seen that for small underwater blasting operations, the use of safety fuse, and Cordtex is the most practical. When drilled shot-holes are used underwater, or the charge has been inserted under rocks or a wreck, it is not necessary to employ the surface practice of 'stemming' or 'tamping'. The primer cartridge must be in good contact with the cartridges that make up the bulk charge.

Often large boulders or pinnacles of rock jut up from the rock bed. There are two methods of dealing with them. They can

Underwater Blasting

often be removed by plaster shots. These consist of a charge of explosive placed on the surface of the rock. Extra confinement of the charge is obtained if it can be placed under the rock. To deal with larger boulders it will be necessary to drill holes into the rock. The hole should only be slightly larger than the cartridges (at least $\frac{1}{8}$ in clearance all round is desirable). The primer cartridge with its detonator goes in last. This is known as 'pop' shooting'.

In wreck dispersal and salvage work, vessels often have to be flattened down. A 1,000-ton vessel of wood or metal construction would require charges in the region of 200 lb in the fore part of the ship, 300 lb aft and 500 lb amidships. The heavy surge of water resulting from the explosion assists in levelling down the sides and plates. In addition, further explosive may be required to level down the boilers, and a 50-lb case of explosive placed through the firebox and as near the centre of the boiler as possible is usually sufficient.

Larger steel ships cannot be broken up in such a simple manner. Concentrated charges are of little value, except in breaking out the stern frame and the bows, as they only act locally. In these cases it is necessary to use long charges of explosive made up in canvas hose or rubber tubing to cut through the deck. Similar charges should also be placed on the hull of the wreck to cut through the hull plates. The wreck will then be found to bulge out and flatten down considerably.

The explosive used for this work is normally submarine blasting gelatine. Charges 60 ft in length are not uncommon and it is necessary to weight the charges at intervals along the length in order to lower them into position. Divers must ensure that the charges are in continuous contact with the hull.

The diameter of the charge depends on the thickness of the plate to be cut and the depth of the water. In shallow water the following will probably give the required results:

Thickness of plate (in)	Diameter of cartridge (in)
$\frac{3}{8}$	$1\frac{3}{4}$
$\frac{1}{2}$	2
$\frac{3}{4}$	$2\frac{1}{2}$
1	$3\frac{1}{4}$

In heads of water greater than 100 ft the corresponding diameters will have to be increased.

Near the end of the last century, Professor Munroe discovered that if a cavity were made in an explosive charge and then placed against a surface, the penetration produced in the surface on detonating the explosive charge was greater than if the explosive had been applied to the surface as a solid charge. This is termed the 'Munroe effect'. Devices incorporating this effect are generally referred to as shaped charges.

The charges can be made up inside a cone, inside a semi-cylinder, or inside an elongated angle-piece of metal, the angle at the apex being 80 degrees, the latter type being called a stook charge. The stook charge is used for cutting and is made up in 1, 2 and 3 ft lengths, and is loaded with 1 to 2 lb of explosive per foot of run.

Piles are divided into three main types, namely, wooden piling, tubular steel piling and sheet steel piling. The method of dealing with the first two types is relatively the same and that is to tie a necklace charge round the pile at the selected height for cutting. A necklace charge is a continuous charge of explosive, the cartridges being placed end to end, and can be made up in either a length of hose or by attaching the cartridges to a length of cord. In the case of wooden piles of 12 in diameter, cartridges of $1\frac{1}{2}$ in are required. The size required to cut tubular steel piles can be determined by applying the rule for wreck cutting.

To cut off a pile cleanly, it is sometimes better to place two separate charges on either side, one 3 in above the other to produce a shearing action.

There is an alternative method of dealing with wooden piles, and that is to bore an inclined hole down into each pile with a wood auger, until it is two-thirds of the way through. The hole is then charged with explosive cartridges, a 12-in pile requiring from 12 to 16 oz.

Obstructions on a soft bottom can often be sunk into the mud by firing a small charge underneath them.

ROCK EXCAVATION

Rock excavation underwater requires suitable drilling equip-

Underwater Blasting

ment, usually mounted on a raft or pontoon. As in dry rock blasting, the method is to establish a free face on one side of the area to be blasted and then take off successive lifts of rock parallel to the free face. Owing to the water pressure on the free face the shotholes must be drilled closer together, and the explosives charges required are heavier than when blasting in the open.

For the same reason shotholes should be drilled well below grade. Usually it is preferable to drill as far below grade as the spacing between the holes. This makes sure that the rock is blasted to the required depth and avoids the costly and difficult operation of redrilling any incompletely blasted section.

Drilling is usually done through pipes which have been sunk through the overlying silt to the rock below. If possible these pipes should extend above water level, this greatly facilitating subsequent charging, since the explosive cartridges can be pushed down into position into the shotholes as in normal blasting practice.

The charges required vary from 1 lb to 4 lb of explosive per cubic yard of rock, depending on the depth of water, depth of breakage required and the hardness of the rock. For example, in the removal of a 12 ft thick layer of rock, using $2\frac{1}{2}$ in diameter holes the spacing should be 5 ft from the face and 5 ft apart, and the depth about 17 ft. If a drill is available to drill holes of say 6–8 in diameter, the hole spacing can be increased to 10 ft and the depth should be increased to 22 ft. If the debris is to be removed by a dredger it is not usually advisable to exceed 10 ft between the holes, otherwise there may be insufficient fragmentation.

REMOVAL OF SAND AND SILT

Sand or silt can often readily be removed from silted-up channels, and new channels cut through sandbanks, by blasting. The normal method is to blast a single row of holes along the centre line of the required channel, but for wide channels it may be necessary to fire several rows of holes. It is important to take maximum advantage of the water flow to scour out the loosened sand or silt. The blasting should be done at the time of maximum flow on an ebbing tide, and if possible water should be dammed upstream and released immediately after blasting. The primed explosive charges are pushed down into the silt and fired simultaneously, using either an electric detonator for each charge or a main line of Cordtex connected to each charge.

Under favourable conditions the charges may be set off by the propagation method. In this, one charge only is primed with an electric detonator—the other charges are placed close enough to be set off by the shock wave from the adjacent charge.

BLASTING TRENCHES

Blasting is a quick and convenient means of excavating trenches for carrying pipelines or cables across river beds. The complete trench should normally be blasted in one operation, since the excavation will be quickly silted up by the flow of water. Where the river is narrow and shallow with a bed of silt or mud, a suitable method is to prepare a continuous explosives charge made up of bundles of cartridges tied end to end on a rope and weighted to lie on the river bed. The charge should be initiated with a length of Cordtex in close contact with the whole length of the explosives charge.

Where 2 in diameter cartridges can be used, Geophex in Seislok couplers is eminently suitable for this method of blasting, since long rigid columns of explosive can be rapidly assembled. The Cordtex fuse should be threaded into the charge so that each cartridge is pierced at least once by the Cordtex to ensure good initiation. Satisfactory initiation is not always obtained from the Cordtex through the thick cardboard of the couplers.

Depth of trench required (ft)	Explosive density (lb/ft)	Recommended cartridge diameter (in)
2–3	1	$1\frac{7}{8}$
3–4	2	2
4–5	5	$3\frac{1}{4}$
above 5	10	5

Underwater Blasting

Where wide or deep trenches are required, or where hard rock is encountered, it is necessary to drill shotholes in the river bed. For example, a 7 ft deep trench 400 ft long was required to accommodate an 18-in gas main. Two rows of holes were drilled 9 ft deep. The rows were 2 ft apart. The holes in each row were 4 ft 6 in apart and a total charge of 1,000 lb of explosive was used.

Very often a job is complicated by the presence of weed. This can generally be removed by the judicial use of small charges lowered from the surface.

When charging a shothole, insert the cartridges one at a time and squeeze each home gently with a wooden rod. Don't ram or pound the cartridge, or bunch or double them up; use a size suitable for the shothole. Then lower or push the primer cartridge into the hole until it rests against the charge. Don't squeeze the primer cartridge home.

Always use one or more large cartridges, rather than several small ones, and never use a small cartridge as the primer. Put primer cartridges into shotholes with the detonator pointing towards the bulk of the charge. Placing a primer cartridge so that the detonator is at some point in the interior of the charge, has adverse effects on complete and effective detonation.

PRECAUTIONS

Do not place explosives on or near fires, stoves, steampipes or heated bodies, in hot water or steam, or in the direct rays of the sun. With the low-freezing types of explosives now in general use, thawing is not necessary. Cartridges and detonators must always be handled with very great care.

In the UK, a private person may buy and store a small quantity of high explosives and detonators. He must apply to the Chief Officer of Police, who will, providing the applicant is considered a suitable person, issue a certificate authorising the person to keep, for private use and not for sale, a maximum of 10 lb of high explosive or 30 lb of blackpowder (gunpowder), 100 detonators, and safety fuse unlimited. These are the maximum amounts allowed to be kept without having special storage premises licensed by the local authority.

Full information on storing explosives is contained in the ICI booklet, *Explosives—The Sale, Storage and Conveyance by Road.*

The regulations regarding the use and storage of explosive materials vary throughout the world, and it is essential to check with the relevant authority in each country where work is being undertaken.

(*The author is indebted to the Nobel Division of* ICI *Ltd for their assistance in compiling this chapter, and for granting permission to use photographs and information contained in their technical publications.*)

15

SEAMANSHIP FOR DIVERS

THE MAGNETIC COMPASS

NEVER put to sea without a magnetic compass aboard. The only really practical compass at sea is the liquid compass, which remains reasonably steady despite the motion of the boat. A magnetic compass derives its directional properties from the earth's natural magnetic force. The force is of a nature that attracts the northerly seeking end of a freely suspended magnet, so that it points to the north magnetic pole. This does not coincide with the true north pole, and the error is termed the variation. The variation is applied to the compass reading, to obtain the true geographical direction.

The variation at any particular position on earth can be ascertained by examining a nautical chart. In the English Channel the variation is approximately 10 degrees W, so that the magnetic compass will read 'best', that is, the compass will read 10 degrees more than the true direction, and the 10 degrees will have to be deducted. If the variation is E, the compass will read 'least', and to determine the true direction the 10 degrees will have to be added.

It is not 'playing safe' to take two magnetic compasses aboard a small boat, as they may be close enough to attract or repel each other, and then neither of them will be reading correctly. Any mass of metal or electrical apparatus can also deflect a compass needle from its natural magnetic direction. This error is called the deviation of the compass, and it can be allowed for in the case of a fixed compass. With a loose, or a wrist compass, only

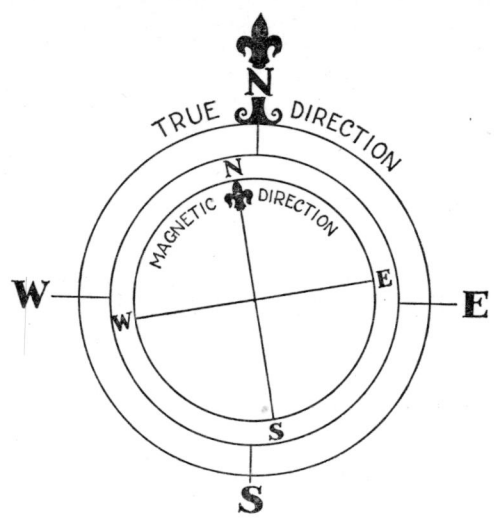

The magnetic compass

take navigational bearings, or set courses, with the compass well away from any disturbing influence.

The steel cylinders of self-contained apparatus deflect the needle of a compass worn on the wrist, and the compass cannot be relied on for underwater navigation. However, a swim-diver on the surface can take a compass bearing of a distant rock or boat, but when taking the bearing he must be in the same horizontal attitude that he will be in on the bottom. If the diver intends walking across the bottom towards the object, then he must take the bearing on the surface when he is in a vertical position. Any relative change of position between the steel cylinder and the compass will alter the amount of error on the compass.

It is difficult to swim underwater following a steady compass course with the compass held in a position so that it can be read. It is much better to pick out a rock which happens to be on the compass course, and then swim to it. On arriving, look at the compass and pick out another object which happens to be on course, and so on.

If mist or fog threatens, the boat crew must fix their position whilst it is still possible, and take a compass bearing of the harbour entrance, or other desired point of return. After the fog has clamped down, rely on your compass; it is much more likely to be right than your instincts.

TIDES AND TIDAL CURRENTS

The moon, revolving round the earth, pulls up a mass of sea-water which causes the level of the open seas to rise and fall vertically twice in twenty-four hours. The sun's gravitational pull also affects the mass of water, but to a much less extent. When the sun and moon exert a pull in the same direction, the high and low tides will be at a maximum and minimum. These are called the spring tides, and occur every full and new moon, that is once every two weeks. When they exert their respective gravitational pull at right angles to each other, the total force is lessened, and the tidal rise and fall will be at a minimum. These are called the neap tides.

Due to the configuration of the land masses, this rise and fall of the sea level also causes a horizontal motion of the sea-water. This is called the tidal current and must not be confused with the rise and fall of the tide. They both affect the diver, but in different ways. A tidal current can handicap a standard diver more than it will a free diver, due mainly to the drag of his air hose and breast rope, and also because his bulky, air-filled suit offers a greater area to the current, especially when in his more usual upright position.

The greater strength of a current is normally at the surface, decreasing somewhat on descent, due to the surface drag of the bottom. A diver may feel conditions are going to be bad, but then finds he can work quite comfortably when lying or kneeling down, or working in the lee of a wreck. The standard diver always has the nuisance of his hose and breast rope which pulls him about in a strong current, and he may decide to make them fast to some substantial structure, with a short length of line, so that he can work more comfortably.

Whilst on the shot rope, the standard diver should endeavour to keep his back to the current, and the shot rope in front of him. This will prevent his hold on the shot rope being broken by the drag of a strong current. The self-contained diver can descend in very strong currents by hanging grimly on to the shot rope and allowing his body to stream down current. He then offers a very small area to the stream, and can complete satisfactorily many jobs that would be impossible with standard gear.

However, most underwater work can be arranged for the slack water period which occurs every six hours. Alternate periods will be low water, and it is usual to take advantage of the shallow water. In the estuary of a river there is a good case for working at high water slack tide, as the river is then full of clean sea-water. Visibility can be many times better than at low water, when all the mud of the river has been brought down, and an area of thick water extends well out of sea.

Tide tables are available in several forms, local tidal information being available from ship or yacht chandlers, bookshops, etc in the district. Comprehensive tables, which include all coasts of Britain, America and important ports elsewhere, will be found in Reed's or Brown's *Nautical Almanacs*, published annually. It will be seen from the tables that not only the times of high and low water vary from place to place, but also the height of high water.

Coastal charts indicate the depth of water at low water spring tides in fathoms. One fathom equals 6 ft. Large scale harbour plans indicate the depth in feet. The units of measurement are always shown on the chart or plan, and should be verified when planning a descent.

It is the small figures which denote the depth, and this sounding often includes letters which indicate the nature of the bottom. The indicated depth is the depth of water over that spot at mean low water spring tides, so that during neap tides there will be a greater depth of water. Spring tides have the greatest rise and fall, and neap tides a lesser rise and fall. Spring tides therefore give the shallowest water over a given spot, but spring tides also have the strongest tidal currents which stir up the bottom and reduce the visibility underwater.

On the whole, neap tides with their weaker currents and clearer water are more favourable for both sporting and salvage diver. The heights of high water given in the tables are the

Seamanship for Divers

heights above the chart datum, and the chart datum is low water mean spring tides—the level from which the depths shown on the chart are measured.

The tide runs for six hours approximately (6 hours 12 minutes) from low water to high water, or high water to low water. During the first hour it will rise or fall 1/12 of the height between high water and low water, during the second hour 2/12, third hour 3/12, fourth hour 3/12, fifth hour 2/12, and sixth hour 1/12.

To determine the approximate depth of water over a given spot on the chart at high water, add the height of the tide in feet, to the depth shown on the chart in fathoms or feet. At low water spring tides, the depth will be the depth shown on the chart. At any other tide the range of the tide will not be the difference from the chart datum to high water, but the height of the tide from low water to high water.

Admiralty tide tables give the height of low water above chart datum as well as high water, and this being the range of the tide, it is only necessary to apply the twelfth rule to obtain the depth of water over any given spot. When using tables which do not show height of low water, it can be assumed that low water is the same height above low water spring tides (shown on chart as soundings), as the high water is below the high water spring tides, which can be picked out roughly from the tide tables.

Therefore, to find the depth of water at a given time over a certain spot, use the twelfth rule to determine the rise or fall of the tide from low or high water. From this the height of water above low water is determined, to which is added the height of low water above chart datum, and the depth of water shown on the chart.

The above method is only an approximation, but as tidal prediction is an inexact science, due to weather conditions prevailing, there is little point in working for greater accuracy.

Although tidal currents are a great nuisance to the diver, they can be used to advantage when exploring with self-contained apparatus. The diver can swim down and then allow the current to sweep him over the bottom, his boat attendant staying close to his bubbles. The diver must keep a sharp look-out down current, as he may be swept into an obstruction with some force. If the surface is so rough that there is any doubt about the atten-

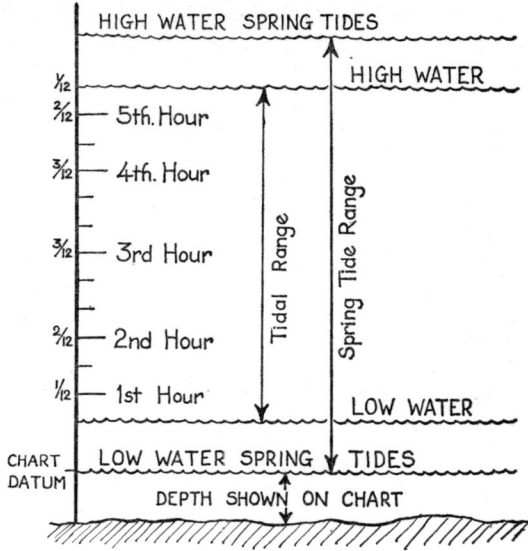

Rise and fall of tides

dant keeping track of the diver's bubbles, use a line, as the boat and diver could be separated by a considerable distance in the space of half an hour. The boat and diver will then be swept along together. The attendant should hold the line, with plenty of slack available, so that in the event of the diver deciding to stop or being caught up in an obstruction, the attendant can heave overboard the slack, hanging on to the bare end, whilst he anchors the boat.

POSITION AT SEA

Position fixing in coastal waters can be easily accomplished by taking transit bearings and compass bearings. A transit bearing is an imaginary line running through two terrestrial objects and the observer. Two such bearings will give an absolute fix of position. The two bearings should have an angle between them as near to 90 degrees as possible.

Having noted that the boat is in line with two prominent objects, the observer identifies them on the chart and draws a line through them continuing the line well past the position in which the boat must be. As the boat must be somewhere on this line, it is called a position line. The point at which a second position line crosses the first will indicate the position of the boat and is termed a 'fix'.

When there are no convenient transits, two compass bearings can be taken on prominent objects. Having been corrected to true bearings, and the reciprocals laid off on the chart from the objects observed, they will form a 'fix'. Three bearings will form a small triangle in which the observer must be.

The best investment is a liquid magnetic compass with three figure notation, 0 degrees to 360 degrees. An ex-aircraft hand-bearing compass is ideal for taking bearings, but is not suitable as a steering compass. In the past, seamen have calibrated compass cards in points and quarter points, converted them to degrees measured from north and south for magnetic courses or bearings, and three figure notation for true bearings. The modern tendency is to use three figure notation for everything and adding (C), (M) or (T) to indicate whether it is a compass, magnetic or true bearing or course.

BUOYAGE

Important deep water channels are marked at sea, in estuaries or in rivers by navigational buoys. They are marked in relation to the direction of the flood stream, the right hand side of a channel when facing in the direction of the flood stream, being termed the starboard side of the channel. The starboard side of a channel is marked with a conical shaped buoy, the port side by a can buoy (flat topped). When entering an estuary or harbour, conical buoys are kept on the boat's starboard side and can buoys to port, being reversed when leaving or travelling in the direction of the ebb tide.

Spherical buoys mark middle grounds, such as sandbanks in the middle of a channel. All wreck marking buoys must be painted green, with the word WRECK painted in white letters.

It is an offence to make a boat fast to a navigational buoy.

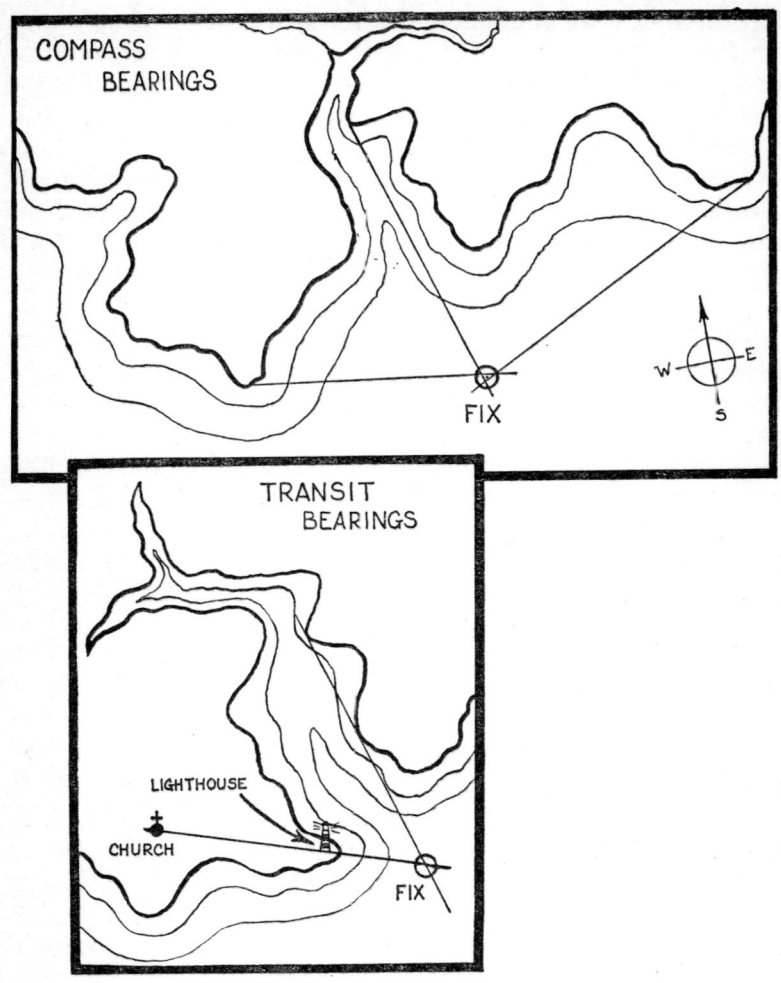

Cross bearings and transit bearings

ROPE

Rope is often made of sisal. It is the cheapest rope, and does its job, but manilla rope is much better. Since the war, little manilla has been available in Britain. The best rope of all, and the strongest, is Italian hemp, but it costs two or three times the price of sisal. Cotton rope should be avoided as it is only a decorative rope. When wet, it kinks badly and loses strength. A useful rope, made from coconut fibre, is called coir or bass rope. It is light and springy, making excellent warps for anchoring and mooring vessels. In recent years man-made fibres such as nylon and terylene have replaced to a large extent the ropes made from natural fibres. The advantages are great strength and resistance to decay, and in addition, some of them are buoyant which means that a diver using them is less likely to be fouled underwater.

When new rope is being taken from a coil it is better to take it from the middle. Right handed rope must be uncoiled anticlockwise, and left handed rope clockwise. It is important to be able to determine which is right handed rope and which is left handed. Holding a length of rope straight out from you, note which way the strands go. The strands of right handed rope run from left to right, and left handed rope from right to left. Right handed rope must be coiled down clockwise, and left handed rope must be coiled down anti-clockwise.

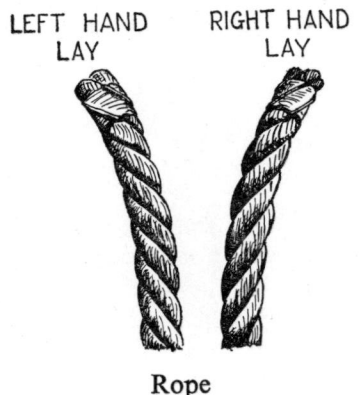

Rope

Before use, the twist will have to be taken out of new rope, or it will kink hopelessly and be impossible to coil down. The easiest method is to stream it behind a boat under way for some time. The size of rope is measured by circumference.

To the diver knots are most important and he must be able to tie and untie them blindfold. A good knot is not necessarily one that is extremely secure, but a knot that is secure and yet can be undone quickly and easily.

The bowline is probably the most useful of all knots, as it never jams and can always be undone, but not with a strain on it. It cannot slip or tighten, and is therefore the knot to use when passing a line round a diver in trouble. A rolling hitch is the knot to use when it is required to hold the standing part of another rope or wire, when the strain on both ropes is in the same direction. It will not slip and can be undone with the strain on either or both ropes. A sheet bend is used when joining a light rope to a heavy rope, or a line to an eye in rope or wire. A round turn and two half hitches will hold securely and yet can be let go with the strain still on. A clove hitch, reef knot and overhand knot will complete the list of essential knots, but other knots and variations of the above can be learned with advantage.

Wire rope is difficult to handle, but its use is essential in the salvage world. It cannot be knotted easily, but it can be hitched loosely several times and the bare end seized back to the standing part. A carrick bend can be used to join two wires together. The breaking strain of 24-strand wire can be determined by squaring the circumference in inches and multiplying by three: breaking strain in tons = circ ^{2} × 3. The working strain is one-fifth of the breaking strain.

* * *

Always keep an eye on the weather when working at sea or in an exposed position. There is not much point in being a first class diver if you are going to sink the works through bad seamanship. You might even have to hire a diver to recover your gear.

Apart from the BBC gale warnings, most harbours and coast-guard stations hoist a visual signal when a gale is expected to develop in the vicinity. The signal is in the form of a black cone 3 ft high and 3 ft wide at the base. If the gale is expected to blow from any direction between north-west through north to east, it will be hoisted with the apex at the top, and if from south-east through south to west, it is hoisted apex down. The signal is lowered when it is expected that there will be a period of at least twelve hours free from gales or high winds.

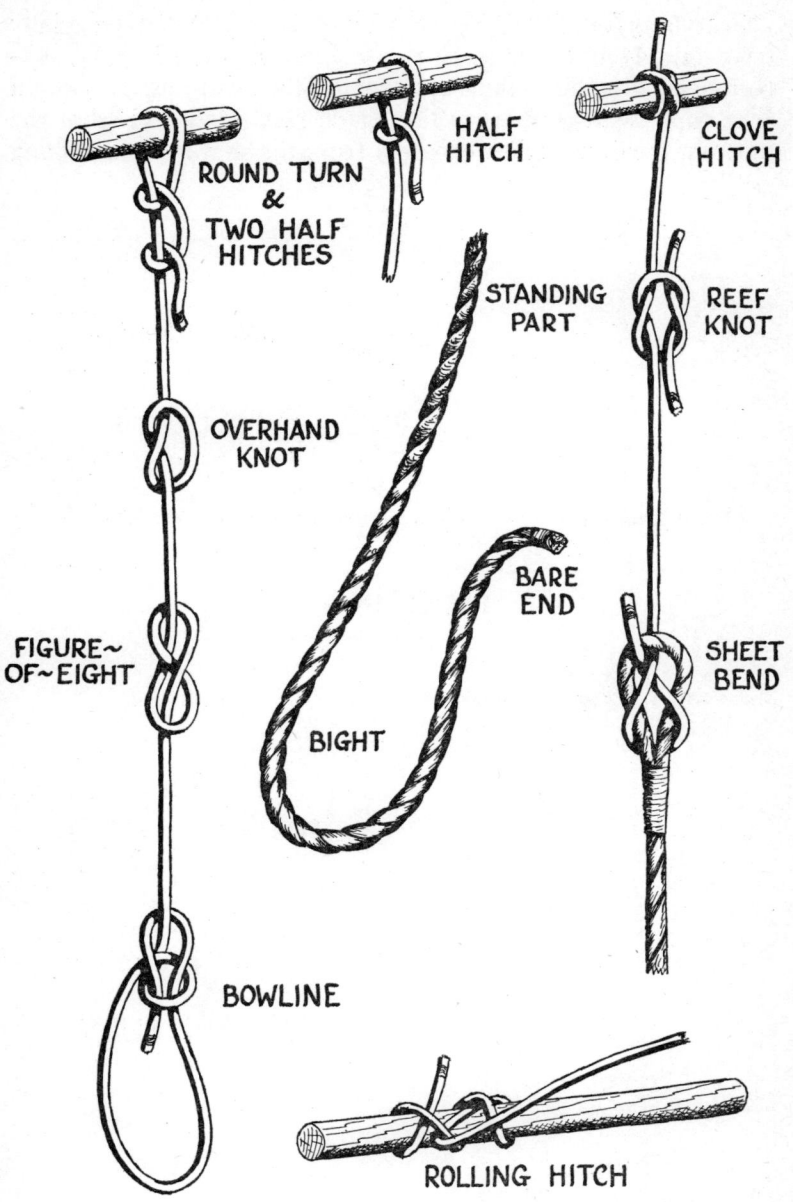

Bends and hitches

Searching for a small object can be quite a problem, especially on a muddy bottom. In this case the swim-diver, using self-contained breathing apparatus has all the advantages. Using a shot rope, with a distance line made fast a few feet from the bottom, the diver swims off away from the shot rope, uncoiling

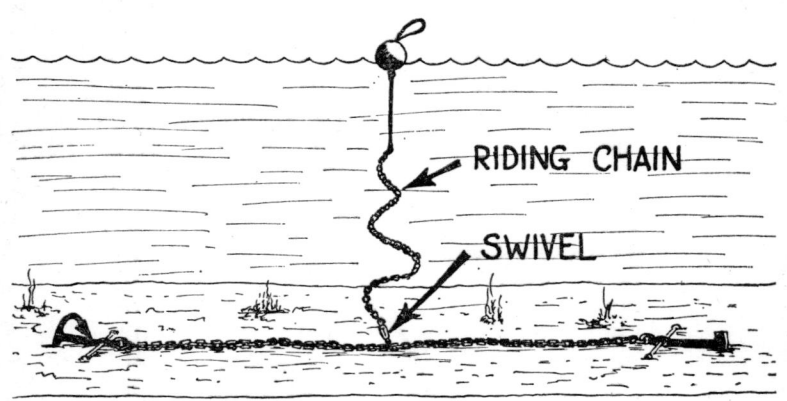

A MOORING

MOORING BUOY

SINGLE 'DEADMAN' MOORING

Moorings

the distance line as he goes. Mark the mud, or take note of some object on the bottom, so that it is known when a complete circle of search has been completed at that radius. Then, depending on the visibility, move several feet inwards, coiling up the slack distance line, and complete another circle, and so on, until reaching the shot. In this way, every inch of the area can be examined visually.

With a larger object, like an outboard engine, whose position may be in some doubt, it is better for a dinghy to tow the diver systematically over the area of search, the diver hanging on to a suitably weighted line. The diver ballasts himself light, by nearly the amount on the end of the line. He can then glide effortlessly up hill and down dale, covering a large area without becoming exhausted, and can give his whole attention to searching. The assistant rowing the dinghy must make sure the diver is covering the whole area, which is quite different from the boat covering the area, due to the length of line out.

The diver should arrange to have a little slack coiled up, so that if the object turns up some distance to one side, he can let go the slack, and the extra scope will allow him to reach the object. He must then hitch the line to the object before the slack is taken up. It is possible to work out several variations of searching, but they must all be systematic, as casual searches rarely pay off.

Sunken moorings can be completely covered in a few days if the bottom is soft mud or sand. If the position is known by a foot or two, the diver can grope about for them with a stiff bent

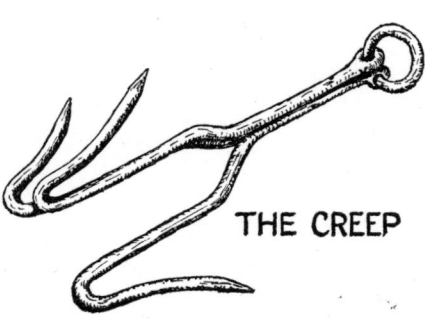

THE CREEP

rod, but if the position is doubtful, it is better to try and foul them by dragging a creep or grapnel across the bottom. Having fouled the ground chain, the diver can then descend and by following the ground chain along, recover the lost rising chain.

When searching for a wreck, the same procedure is followed. The 'creep' is ideal, as it will foul a wire, rail, or small spar very easily.

16

ARTIFICIAL RESPIRATION

THE most efficient method of resuscitation, and certainly the easiest, is the mouth-to-mouth method, and the next best is Eve's Rocking Method. The Schafer, Holger-Nielson, and Silvester's methods all have disadvantages, and being so very inefficient should not be attempted. Mouth-to-mouth resuscitation supplies up to twelve times the volume of air averaged by experts using the other methods.

As mouth-to-mouth resuscitation may be considered objectionable, an ingenious pocket-sized device called a Resuscitating Tube is now widely available. Designed to simplify the mouth-to-mouth technique and make it even more effective, this small S-shaped plastic tube has proved so easy to use that eighty-seven untrained laymen in one experimental test were able, after the briefest of demonstrations, to insert it correctly and start successful resuscitation within 5 to 40 seconds. Moreover, the airway, which combines a mouthpiece for the rescuer with a breathing tube for the victim, eliminates the direct oral contact. These airways were invented by Dr Peter Safar and Captain M. C. McMahon.

If the airway is not immediately available, or cannot be inserted because of a tightly closed jaw, start direct mouth-to-mouth breathing immediately. In children under three years of age, always use direct mouth-to-mouth breathing. Mouth-to-mouth resuscitation, with or without an airway, has an extra life-saving advantage as it avoids the danger of the tongue of the victim sagging against the back of his throat and blocking the air passage.

With this new technique, the victim's head must be tilted back and the lower jaw must be tilted out. The backward tilt of the head unkinks the air passage, and the jutting jaw pulls the tongue forward. Authorities say that some unconscious victims will be saved simply by holding the head and jaw in this position, which permits spontaneous breathing. A resuscitation tube helps by automatically keeping the tongue forward.

With the old 'prone pressure' resuscitation, the first-aider was in effect only 'exhaling' for the victim—pressing air out of the chest cavity and hoping it would refill by suction. In the mouth-to-mouth method, he is doing the opposite, that is, blowing air into the oxygen starved lungs.

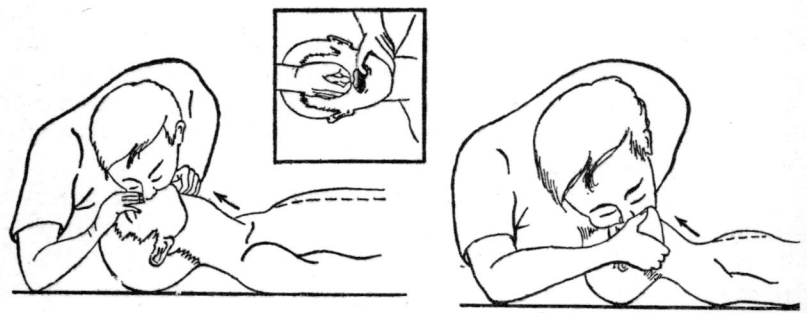

Mouth-to-mouth method of resuscitation: (*left*) in adults; (*right*) in children or in adults with a tight jaw

The first-aider's exhaled breath contains an extra percentage of carbon dioxide (CO_2) which activates the victim's own respiratory centre in the brain and actually promotes his own breathing, and there is still 80 to 90 per cent as much oxygen as in fresh air, which is more than enough required.

MOUTH-TO-MOUTH METHOD IN ADULTS

Insert thumb of your left hand between the victim's teeth. Hold the jaw upwards so that head is tilted backward. Close the victim's nostril with your right hand. Take a deep breath and place your mouth tightly over the victim's mouth and your own thumbs. Blow forcefully enough to make victim's chest rise. Repeat inflations every three or four seconds.

Artificial Respiration 177

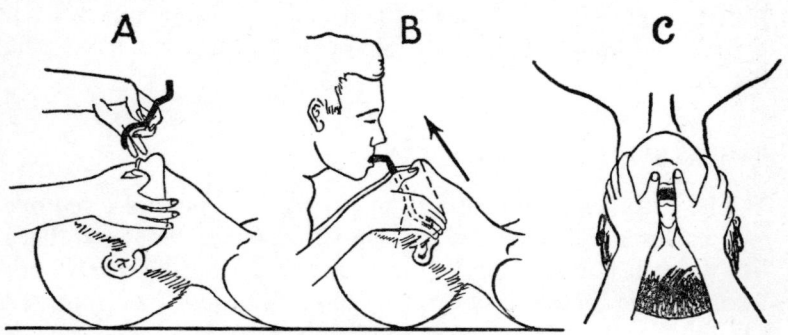

A, insertion of airway; B, mouth-to-airway technique;
C, position of rescuer's hands

MOUTH-TO-MOUTH METHOD IN CHILDREN
(OR IN ADULTS WITH TIGHT JAW)

Grasp the angles of the child's jaw at the ear lobes with both hands, and lift up forcibly so that the head is tilted backward. Push the child's lower lip towards the chin with your thumbs. Never let the chin sag. Take a breath and place your mouth tightly over child's mouth. (For small children cover both mouth and nose.)

Blow air in gently until chest moves, then take your mouth off and let him exhale passively. Repeat inflations once every two or three seconds. (Note: For adults, blow forcefully. For a child blow gently, and for an infant use puffs.)

When an unconscious person is breathing, it is important to hold his head tilted backwards and jaw raised forward to keep his air passageway open until he is conscious.

EVE'S ROCKING METHOD

This is the next best form of artificial respiration, but it requires a short ladder, door or wide board. The victim is placed face downwards and the type of stretcher used is then rocked twelve times a minute, see-saw fashion, starting with an angle of 40 degrees each way. The wrists and ankles are secured to the four corners of the stretcher. The abdominal viscera forces the diaphragm up and down, inducing an efficient respiratory action. Small children and babies can be rocked in the arms, as they lie face downwards.

TREATMENT FOR SHOCK

Whilst artificial respiration is in progress, if possible, remove wet clothing and cover the person with warmed blankets. Place hot water bottles beside the limbs and body, but be careful not to burn the patient. Only after consciousness has returned should any attempt be made to offer hot drinks.

DECOMPRESSION TABLES

STOPS REQUIRED FOR DEPTH AND DURATION OF DESCENT

AIR DECOMPRESSION

Depth not exceeding (feet)	Duration time leaving surface to beginning of ascent (mins)	Stoppages (mins)						
		80 ft	70 ft	60 ft	50 ft	40 ft	30 ft	20 ft	10 ft
30	No limit	—	—	—	—	—	—	—	—
40	135	—	—	—	—	—	—	—	—
	165	—	—	—	—	—	—	—	5
	195	—	—	—	—	—	—	—	10
	225	—	—	—	—	—	—	—	15
	255	—	—	—	—	—	—	—	20
	330	—	—	—	—	—	—	—	25
	390	—	—	—	—	—	—	—	30
	660	—	—	—	—	—	—	—	35
	over 660	—	—	—	—	—	—	—	40
50	105	—	—	—	—	—	—	—	5
	120	—	—	—	—	—	—	—	10
	135	—	—	—	—	—	—	—	15
	145	—	—	—	—	—	—	—	20
	160	—	—	—	—	—	—	—	25
	170	—	—	—	—	—	—	5	25
	190	—	—	—	—	—	—	5	30
	240	—	—	—	—	—	—	10	40
	360	—	—	—	—	—	—	30	40
	450	—	—	—	—	—	—	35	40
	over 450	—	—	—	—	—	—	35	45
60	70	—	—	—	—	—	—	—	5
	80	—	—	—	—	—	—	5	5

Depth not exceeding (feet)	Duration time leaving surface to beginning of ascent (mins)	Stoppages (mins)							
		80 ft	70 ft	60 ft	50 ft	40 ft	30 ft	20 ft	10 ft
60	90	—	—	—	—	—	—	5	10
	100	—	—	—	—	—	—	5	15
	110	—	—	—	—	—	—	5	20
	120	—	—	—	—	—	—	5	25
	130	—	—	—	—	—	—	5	30
	140	—	—	—	—	—	—	10	30
	150	—	—	—	—	—	—	10	40
	160	—	—	—	—	—	—	15	40
	180	—	—	—	—	—	—	20	40
	200	—	—	—	—	—	5	30	40
70	55	—	—	—	—	—	—	—	5
	60	—	—	—	—	—	—	5	5
	70	—	—	—	—	—	—	5	10
	75	—	—	—	—	—	—	5	15
	85	—	—	—	—	—	—	5	20
	90	—	—	—	—	—	—	5	25
	95	—	—	—	—	—	5	5	25
	105	—	—	—	—	—	5	5	35
	120	—	—	—	—	—	5	10	40
	135	—	—	—	—	—	5	20	45
	150	—	—	—	—	—	5	30	45
80	40	—	—	—	—	—	—	—	5
	50	—	—	—	—	—	—	5	5
	55	—	—	—	—	—	—	5	10
	60	—	—	—	—	—	—	5	15
	70	—	—	—	—	—	—	5	20
	75	—	—	—	—	—	—	5	25
	80	—	—	—	—	—	5	5	30
	90	—	—	—	—	—	5	10	35
	105	—	—	—	—	—	5	20	40
	120	—	—	—	—	5	5	30	45
	140	—	—	—	—	5	10	35	50
	160	—	—	—	—	10	30	40	50
90	40	—	—	—	—	—	—	5	5
	45	—	—	—	—	—	—	5	10
	50	—	—	—	—	—	—	5	15
	55	—	—	—	—	—	—	5	20
	60	—	—	—	—	—	5	5	20
	65	—	—	—	—	—	5	5	25
	70	—	—	—	—	—	5	10	30
	75	—	—	—	—	—	5	15	30
	80	—	—	—	—	—	5	20	35
	90	—	—	—	—	—	5	25	40

Decompression Tables

Depth not exceeding (feet)	Duration time leaving surface to beginning of ascent (mins)	Stoppages (mins)							
		80 ft	70 ft	60 ft	50 ft	40 ft	30 ft	20 ft	10 ft
90	100	—	—	—	—	—	5	30	45
	110	—	—	—	—	5	15	35	45
	120	—	—	—	—	5	20	35	50
100	30	—	—	—	—	—	—	5	5
	35	—	—	—	—	—	—	5	10
	40	—	—	—	—	—	—	5	15
	45	—	—	—	—	—	—	5	20
	50	—	—	—	—	—	5	5	20
	55	—	—	—	—	—	5	5	25
	60	—	—	—	—	—	5	10	30
	70	—	—	—	—	—	5	20	35
	75	—	—	—	—	5	5	20	40
	80	—	—	—	—	5	5	30	40
	90	—	—	—	—	5	15	30	45
	105	—	—	—	—	5	25	35	50
110	25	—	—	—	—	—	—	5	5
	30	—	—	—	—	—	—	5	10
	35	—	—	—	—	—	—	5	15
	40	—	—	—	—	—	—	5	20
	45	—	—	—	—	—	5	5	20
	50	—	—	—	—	—	5	10	25
	55	—	—	—	—	—	5	15	30
	60	—	—	—	—	—	5	20	35
	65	—	—	—	—	5	5	20	40
	70	—	—	—	—	5	10	20	45
	75	—	—	—	—	5	15	25	45
	80	—	—	—	—	5	20	30	45
	90	—	—	—	5	5	20	40	45
	100	—	—	—	5	10	25	40	50
120	25	—	—	—	—	—	—	5	5
	30	—	—	—	—	—	—	5	15
	35	—	—	—	—	—	—	5	20
	40	—	—	—	—	—	5	5	25
	45	—	—	—	—	—	5	10	25
	50	—	—	—	—	—	5	15	30
	55	—	—	—	—	5	5	20	35
	60	—	—	—	—	5	10	25	40
	70	—	—	—	—	5	20	30	45
	75	—	—	—	5	5	20	35	45
	80	—	—	—	5	10	25	35	45
	90	—	—	—	5	15	30	40	50
	100	—	—	5	5	20	35	45	55

Depth not exceeding (feet)	Duration time leaving surface to beginning of ascent (mins)	Stoppages (mins)							
		80 ft	70 ft	60 ft	50 ft	40 ft	30 ft	20 ft	10 ft
130	20	—	—	—	—	—	—	5	5
	25	—	—	—	—	—	—	5	10
	30	—	—	—	—	—	—	5	20
	35	—	—	—	—	—	5	5	20
	40	—	—	—	—	—	5	10	25
	45	—	—	—	—	5	5	15	30
	50	—	—	—	—	5	5	20	35
	55	—	—	—	—	5	10	25	40
	60	—	—	—	—	5	15	30	45
	70	—	—	—	5	10	20	30	50
	75	—	—	—	5	15	25	40	50
	80	—	—	—	5	20	30	45	50
	90	—	—	5	5	25	40	45	50
	100	—	5	5	15	30	40	45	50
140	10	—	—	—	—	—	—	—	5
	15	—	—	—	—	—	—	5	5
	20	—	—	—	—	—	—	5	10
	25	—	—	—	—	—	—	5	15
	30	—	—	—	—	—	5	5	20
	35	—	—	—	—	—	5	10	25
	40	—	—	—	—	5	5	15	30
	45	—	—	—	—	5	10	15	35
	50	—	—	—	—	5	15	20	40
	55	—	—	—	5	5	15	25	45
	60	—	—	—	5	5	20	35	45
	65	—	—	—	5	10	25	40	45
	70	—	—	—	5	15	30	40	50
	75	—	—	5	5	20	30	45	50
	80	—	—	5	10	20	35	45	50
	85	—	—	5	15	25	40	45	50
	95	—	5	5	20	35	40	45	50
150	10	—	—	—	—	—	—	—	5
	15	—	—	—	—	—	—	5	5
	20	—	—	—	—	—	—	5	15
	25	—	—	—	—	—	5	5	20
	30	—	—	—	—	—	5	10	25
	35	—	—	—	—	5	5	10	30
	40	—	—	—	—	5	10	15	35
	45	—	—	—	—	5	15	20	40
	50	—	—	—	5	5	15	25	45
	55	—	—	—	5	10	20	30	50
	60	—	—	—	5	15	25	35	50
	65	—	—	5	5	15	30	40	50
	70	—	—	5	10	20	30	45	50
	75	—	—	5	15	25	35	45	50
	80	—	5	5	20	30	40	45	50
	85	—	5	10	25	35	40	45	50

Decompression Tables

Depth not exceeding (feet)	Duration time leaving surface to beginning of ascent (mins)	Stoppages (mins)							
		80 ft	70 ft	60 ft	50 ft	40 ft	30 ft	20 ft	10 ft
160	10	—	—	—	—	—	—	5	5
	15	—	—	—	—	—	—	5	10
	20	—	—	—	—	—	5	5	15
	25	—	—	—	—	—	5	10	20
	30	—	—	—	—	5	5	10	25
	35	—	—	—	—	5	10	15	30
	40	—	—	—	—	5	10	20	40
	45	—	—	—	5	5	15	25	45
	50	—	—	—	5	10	20	30	45
	55	—	—	—	5	15	25	40	45
	60	—	—	5	5	20	25	40	50
	65	—	—	5	10	20	35	45	50
	70	—	—	5	15	25	40	45	50
	75	—	5	5	20	30	40	45	50
	80	—	5	10	25	35	40	45	50
	85	—	5	15	30	40	45	45	50
170	10	—	—	—	—	—	—	5	5
	15	—	—	—	—	—	—	5	10
	20	—	—	—	—	—	5	5	15
	25	—	—	—	—	—	5	10	25
	30	—	—	—	—	5	5	15	30
	35	—	—	—	—	5	10	20	35
	40	—	—	—	5	5	15	25	35
	45	—	—	—	5	10	20	30	40
	50	—	—	5	5	10	25	35	45
	55	—	—	5	5	15	30	40	50
	60	—	—	5	10	20	35	45	50
	65	—	5	5	15	25	35	45	50
	70	—	5	10	15	30	40	45	50
	75	—	5	15	20	35	45	45	50
	80	5	5	20	25	40	45	45	50
180	10	—	—	—	—	—	—	5	5
	15	—	—	—	—	—	5	5	10
	20	—	—	—	—	—	5	10	15
	25	—	—	—	—	5	5	10	25
	30	—	—	—	—	5	10	15	35
	35	—	—	—	5	5	15	20	40
	40	—	—	—	5	10	20	25	45
	45	—	—	5	5	10	25	35	45
	50	—	—	5	5	15	30	40	50
	55	—	—	5	10	20	35	45	50
	60	—	5	5	15	25	40	45	50
	65	—	5	10	20	30	40	45	50
	70	—	5	15	25	35	45	45	50
	75	5	5	20	30	40	45	45	50

Depth not exceeding (feet)	Duration time leaving surface to beginning of ascent (mins)	Stoppages (mins)							
		80 ft	70 ft	60 ft	50 ft	40 ft	30 ft	20 ft	10 ft
190	10	—	—	—	—	—	—	5	5
	15	—	—	—	—	—	5	5	15
	20	—	—	—	—	—	5	10	20
	25	—	—	—	—	5	5	15	25
	30	—	—	—	5	5	10	20	35
	35	—	—	—	5	5	15	30	45
	40	—	—	5	5	10	20	35	45
	45	—	—	5	5	15	25	40	50
	50	—	—	5	10	20	30	45	50
	55	—	5	5	15	25	35	45	50
	60	—	5	10	20	30	40	45	50
	65	5	5	10	25	35	45	45	50
	70	5	10	15	30	40	45	45	50
200	10	—	—	—	—	—	—	5	10
	15	—	—	—	—	—	5	5	15
	20	—	—	—	—	5	5	10	20
	25	—	—	—	—	5	10	15	30
	30	—	—	—	5	5	15	20	40
	35	—	—	—	5	10	20	30	45
	40	—	—	5	5	15	25	40	45
	45	—	—	5	10	20	30	45	50
	50	—	5	5	15	25	35	45	50
	55	—	5	10	20	30	40	45	50
	60	5	5	10	25	35	45	45	50

Warning: The factor of safety is small and it is essential to keep well within the time limits of the table.

The tabulated duration is the time from leaving the surface to the time of commencing the ascent. If the time spent on the bottom exceeds the tabulated time, the next longer time is used. The tabulated times must not be exceeded.

At no time should the ascent exceed 25 ft per minute. The last 10 ft should take 1 minute.

A second deep dive within a 12 hour period must be treated as a continuation of the first dive, and decompression carried out for the sum of the periods.

Decompression Tables

Decompression periods can be divided by 2·5 when using pure oxygen. Oxygen must not be used below 30 ft.

No stops are required at the following depths, providing these periods are not exceeded:

30 ft	Unlimited
40 ,,	120 min
50 ,,	78 ,,
60 ,,	55 ,,
70 ,,	43 ,,
80 ,,	35 ,,
90 ,,	30 ,,
100 ,,	25 ,,
110 ,,	20 ,,
120 ,,	18 ,,
130 ,,	15 ,,

Appendix

MANUFACTURERS OF DIVING EQUIPMENT

THERE are several manufacturers who can supply diving apparatus in its various forms. The apparatus differs in design details, but works basically the same way, and can be divided into three classes.

1. *Standard Diving Gear*   This is what is called 'hard hat' in the United States, which is most descriptive, the rigid helmet normally being supplied with air or a mixture of gases from the surface although self-contained versions have been manufactured, the diver carrying cylinders of air or other respirable gases on his back.

    This type of gear can be supplied by Messrs Siebe, Gorman & Co Ltd, Davis Road, Chessington, Surrey, England. Diving Equipment & Supply Co (DESCO), 234 North Broadway, Milwaukee 2, Wisconsin, USA, Morse Diving Equipment Co, 470 Atlantic Avenue, Boston 10, Mass USA,, and Miller-Dunn Co 2517 NW, 21st Terrace, Miami, Fla, USA.

2. *Oxygen Breathing Apparatus*   This type of closed circuit apparatus is manufactured in Britain by Messrs Dunlop & Co and Siebe, Gorman & Co Ltd. In the USA by DESCO and the Morse Diving Equipment Co and in Europe by Draeger in Germany, and Pirelli and Cressi in Italy.

3. *Compressed Air Apparatus* (*aqualung*)   This apparatus is used by both amateur and professional divers, usually as self-contained apparatus. Versions of this demand valve controlled equipment are available with a surface supply of air, through light pressure hose, to the diver, the only difference in operation being that the diver is not completely free.

Many versions are manufactured in Britain and overseas by the following concerns: Siebe, Gorman & Co Ltd, which includes the Heinke range, Submarine Products Ltd of Hexham, Northumberland, England; US Divers Co, Los Angeles, Calif USA; Nemrod, Spain; Draeger, Germany; and La Spirotechnique, France. Messrs Dunlop's manufacture the Royal Naval SABA compressed air breathing apparatus, which is very expensive for civilian use.

Most of the above manufacturers can also supply compressors, decompression chambers, recompression chambers, dresses, and frogman type swimsuits, together with ancilliary equipment required by the shallow water and deepsea diver.

Midland Diving Equipment Ltd, No 2 Unit Freehold Street, Leicester, England, manufacture cylinder valves, manifolds, adaptors etc, and supply compressors and compressed air breathing apparatus, suits etc.

DIVING DATA

1 cu ft of fresh water weighs 62·5 lb
1 cu ft of salt water weighs 64 lb
1 atmosphere equals 14·7 lb per sq in
35 cu ft of salt water weigh 1 ton
1 ton of salt water equals 219 imperial gallons
1 ton of fresh water equals 224 imperial gallons
The surface area of an average man's body equals 2,100 sq in
1 lb of fresh water equals 27·6 cu in
1 lb of fresh water equals ·1 imperial gallon
1 imperial gallon of fresh water weighs 10 lb
Atmospheric air contains in volume: 79·1 per cent nitrogen; 20·9 per cent oxygen; ·03 per cent carbon dioxide (CO_2)
A standard diver requires approximately 1·5 cu ft of air at the surface, and an extra 1·5 cu ft for every 33 ft of depth
 A swimming diver using demand valve apparatus requires $\frac{\text{Depth} + 1}{33}$ in cu ft of air at atmospheric pressure
A swimming diver using oxygen breathing apparatus requires approx 1 litre per minute

INDEX

Absolute fix, 167
Air consumption, 48
Air cylinders, 32, 37
Air embolism, 20
Air hose, 61, 68
Air supply, 73
Alumina, 76
Ambient pressure, 15
Ammonium nitrate, 139
Anoxia, 28, 58
Anti-flash valve, 137
Aqualung, 31, 34, 40
Aqualung training, 40
Arcing, 137
Arctic Sea, 124
Arc-welding, 137
Arterioles, 26
Artificial respiration, 175
Asphyxia, 23
Asphyxiation, 22
Atlantic, 100, 124, 127
Atmospheres absolute, 22
Atmospheric air, 22, 28
Atmospheric pressure, 13, 22
Auger, 130
Azores, 100

Back firing, 134
Bass, 109
Bass rope, 169
Belts, standard diver, 64
Bends, 23
Birmingham Underwater Explorers Club, 103
Black diving, 83
Black powder, 139
Bladder wrack, 118

Blasting, 139
Blood, 14, 24
Blood stream, 24
Blood transfusion, 30
Blowing up, 66, 70
Bolt firing gun, 132
Bowline, 170, 171
Breathing apparatus, 31
Breathing bag, 55
Breathing chamber, 33
Breathing tube (snorkel), 13, 85
British Oxygen, 33, 76
British Sub-Aqua Club, 103
British Underwater Centre, 38, 51, 76, 92, 96, 142
Buoyage, 167

CABA (compressed air breathing apparatus), 79
Camera case, 119
Canary Islands, 100
Carbon dioxide (CO_2), 13, 14, 22, 28, 29, 32
Carbon monoxide (CO), 23, 29, 76, 77
Carbon monoxide poisoning, 29
Carley float, 86
Carrick bend, 170
Catarrh, 94
Cement, 130
Coast diving, 85
Coastguard, 170
Channel Islands, 100
Charcoal, 76
Charleston, 100
Chart datum, 165
Charts, 164
Chest, 14

Chloroform, 123
Clove hitch, 170, 171
Coir rope, 169
Collar (rubber), 97
Compressed air apparatus, 31, 32-3, 186
Compressed air illness, 23
Compressor, 29, 75
Concrete, 130
Conger, 113
Contents gauge, 34, 43
Convulsions, 23, 28
Cordtex, 142
Cord-weed, 119
Cornwall, 100
Corselet, 59, 61; straps, 63
Crabs, 101, 104
Creep, 173
Crimpers, 141
Crustacea, 101
Cuff rings ('greys' and 'reds'), 63, 88
Cuffs, 97
Cummerbund, 91
Cylinders, HP, 74, 77

Dabs, 113
Deadman mooring, 172
Decompression, 24, 25, 26, 80; chamber SDC, 24, 25, 26; credit, 25; speed, 21; tables, 179
Deep diving, 79, 80
Deep sea diver, 79
Delay detonators, 150, 151
Demand valve, 37, 77
Depth pressures, 21
Detonators, 140
Deviation, 161
Devon, 100
Diaphragm, 33
Dieseling, 76
Differential pressures, 15
Distance line, 65
Diverphone, 60, 65
Diver's belt, 64; boots, 59; dress, 59; gauge, 74; hose, 61; knife, 63; panel, 61; weights, 60
Diving boat, 39, 83; data, 188; ladder, 39, 83; Operations Special Regulations, 51; physiology, 14
Dogfish, 113
Droits (of Admiralty), 187
Dry swim suit, 88, 91, 92

Dunlop, 31, 95

Ear cavity, 14; compensators, 93; drum, 15; plugs, 16, 42
Ebb tide, 167
Electric detonators, 142, 148
Electrodes, 136, 137
Epiglottis, 15, 43
Exploders, 152
Explosives, 32, 139; licence, 159
Eustachian tubes, 14, 15, 43, 44, 92, 95

Face mask, 15, 42
Factory inspector, 51
Fat person, 23
Feed back, 62
Fishes, 101
Fix, 167
Flag (diver's), 50
Flag signals, 49
Flat fish, 109
Floating hose, 61
Flood stream, 167
Flounder, 113
Free ascent, 21, 38, 39, 44

Gale, 170
Gas cutting, 133
Gas cylinder, 32, 33; (Conveyance) Regulations 1931, 33
Gauge, standard diver's, 74
Gelignites, 139
Generator, 136
Geophex, 140
Gloves, 87, 136
'Greys', 63
Grouting, 130
Gun Licence and Firearm Act, 106
Gunpowder, 139
Gurnard, 115

Hand pump, 61, 73
Hand signals, 65
Harpoon guns, 101, 106
Heinke, 31, 93
Helium, 27, 80
Helmet, 59, 60
Hemp, 168
Herring, 115
High pressure cylinders, 74, 77
High water, 165

Index

Hitches, 170, 171
Hood (rubber), 91, 97
Hose, 61
Hydrocarbon oil, 30, 58
Hydrogen, 27, 134
Hydraulic test, 33
Hydrostatic pressure, 22
Hyperventilation, 13

Indian Ocean, 124
Inflatable dinghy, 86
Inlet valve, 61, 69
Inner collar (bib), 62
Isotherm, 100
Italian hemp, 168

Jock strap, 41
John Dory, 115
Joint insulators, 153
Jones, Dr Peter, 26

Kelp, 118
Kerf, 133
Knife (standard), 63
Knots, 170, 171

Lanyards (weight), 63
Latex rubber, 94
Lay (rope), 169
Lean person, 23
Life jacket, CO_2, 38, 39
Linesman (attendant), 64, 66
Lobsters, 101, 102, 103
Longline, 101
Looe Underwater Club, 103
Low water, 165
Lungs, 14

Madeira, 100
Magnetic compass, 161, 162
Manifold, 74, 78
Manilla, 168
Manufacturers, 186
Marine biology, 101
Mediterranean, 100
Mental aberration, 26, 80
Metabolism, 99
Middle ear, 15
Ministry of Agriculture, Fisheries & Food, 103
Misfire, 154

Mixture diving, 28, 80, 84
Monk fish, 115
Mooring, 172; buoy, 172
Mullet, 101, 109
'Munroe effect', 156
Munroe, Professor, 156

Naphtha, 96
Nausea, 16
Nautical Almanac, 164
Neap tides, 124, 163
Necklace charge, 156
Neoprene, 98
Nervous system, 99
Nicotinic acid, 26
Nitrogen, 56; narcosis, 26, 80
Normandy, 100
North Sea, 124
Nose clip, 15, 41, 64
Nylon, 169

Outlet valve, 64, 65
Over-breathing, 13
Overhand knot, 170, 171
Oxy-acetylene, 133
Oxy-arc cutting, 136
Oxygen, 14, 20, 24, 52, 134; blackout, 29; consumption, 99; poisoning, 24, 27, 56, 58, 81; rebreathing apparatus, 31, 32, 51, 52, 56, 186; starvation, 26; tables, 58; tolerance, 27, 28, 58

Pacific, 124
Panama, 100
Paralysis, 23
Pearler pattern outlet valve, 68
Persian Gulf, 100
Perspex, 123
Photography, 119, 127
Piles, 130, 156
Plaice, 113
Plankton, 124
Pneumatic, 130
Pollack, 101, 109
Porbeagle, 115
Porpoise, 117
Port, 167
Pots (lobster), 101, 117
Pouting, 109
Pressure gauge, 34, 43
Primer cartridge, 142, 159
Pump (hand), 61, 73

Pump (salvage), 131

Ray, 115
Rebreathing apparatus, 31
Recompression chamber, 20
Red Sea, 100
'Reds', 63
Reducing valve, 33, 80
Reef knot, 170, 171
Repetitive dive, 25, 84
Respiration, 33, 99
Respiratory centre, 13
Resuscitation tube, 175, 176
Reverse ear, 19, 91, 92, 94
Rolling hitch, 170, 171
Rope, 168, 169
Royal Navy, 95
Rubber, diaphragm, 34; repairs, 96; skirts, 91; solution, 94, 96, 97
Rupture (eardrum), 15, 16

Safety fuse, 140
Salvage, 131, 192
Salvage pattern outlet valve, 68
Salvus twill material, 87, 96, 97
Sargasso Sea, 124
Sea anemones, 127
Seals, 117
Sea temperature, 100
Sea weeds, 118
Seislock, 140
Self-contained apparatus, 31, 32
Shallow water blackout, 29; diver, 79
Shark, 113
Sheet bend, 170, 171
Shot-firing cable, 153
Shock (treatment of), 178
Shot hole, 159
Shot rope, 41, 92
Shoulder pad, 62
Siebe Gorman, 31, 76, 95
Silica-gel, 76
Silicone oil, 58
Sinking hose, 61
Sinus, 19
Sisal, 168
Six Bolt Helmet, 60
Skin diver (swim-diver), 12, 13
Skin rash, 23
Sladen suit, 88
Snorkel (breathing tube), 12
Soda lime, 52, 55, 56, 57

Sodium nitrate, 139
Sole, 113
Solubility ratio, 24, 27
Soundings, 164
South America, 100
Spear valve, 37
Spinal chord, 23
Spindle, 66
Spit cock, 69
Spring tides, 163
Stage decompression, 24, 25, 27, 80
Standard diving, 32, 59; apparatus, 59, 194; dress, 59, 87, 88, 96
Starboard, 167
Star fish, 127
Stook charge, 156
Studs (weight), 63
Swim-diver, 12, 13
Swim suit (two-piece), 88
Submarine blasting gelatine, 139
Surf, 85
Surface supply, 31, 77

Terylene, 169
Tidal currents, 163
Tide range, 166
Tides, 124, 163
Trammel net, 117
Transit, 166, 168
Twelfth rule, 165

Underclothing, 87
Underwater work, 129
Ushant, 124

Valve, anti-flash, 137; demand, 70, 77; inlet, 61, 69; outlet, 64, 65, 68; outlet, pearler pattern, 68; salvage pattern, 68; reducing, 33, 80; spear, 37
Variation, 161
Vasodilating agent, 26
Venting, 91
Vertigo, 16
Visibility, 83, 124

Washington, 100
Western Isles, 100
West Indies, 100
Wet suit, 87, 98
Wrasse, 101, 109
Wreck, 167,

Zip fastener, 99